Awakening

To Hear The Voice Within

Author: Tammy Wykoff

Editor: Robert J. Wykoff III

Cover Photo: Robert J Wykoff Jr.

Graphics: Carissa Souza

I would like to thank my husband Bob who has supported me on this journey to write this book. He has done all he can to encourage me and be there to help me in any way possible. He helped me to create my front cover. It is a picture he took of the stars and added a person looking at the universe. Thank you so very much.

To my son Robert J. Wykoff, who edited this book. Without his expertise it would not have come together.

To my family who has also supported and helped me on this journey. My son Bob and his fiancé Alissa, my daughter Carissa and her husband John Paul. Thank you for all your kind words and encouragement.

To my wonderful grandchildren Kenzi and Desmond, you always make my life sunshine every day.

I love you, my family, so very much. You make my life happy and complete.

Contents

Awakening to hear the voice within

What I want to teach you through this book is to awaken to hear your inner voice, your inner guidance system, and the inter connection all around you.

I would like to share with you who I am, and what I believe: I believe in the Father, Son, and Holy Spirit. Whatever you believe is part of your journey and where you are along your path. I am not here to judge you. I am here to help you hear the voice within. People are already judged too much in our world. I am here to help where I can and show love to a world that seems to be growing so cold.

I have always felt that I could hear the voice within. When I would pray, answers would come. I just felt it, I knew it, or I was shown through different ways. One way is through books, and there are a number of other ways as well. I'll explain to you in this book how I hear the voice within. Just because I can hear this voice within doesn't mean I always follow what is being shown to me. I have made many of mistakes because I would either ignore the answer or not do what I was shown.

This is a negative part of being human that we all need to get rid of. I wanted to stop doing this and start tuning in on this voice within. I wanted to start doing what I was shown. I'm sure most of us feel this way, but changing our old habits, or set patterns, and doing what we are shown to do can be very hard. It means changing what we know and how we behave. It may also mean that we have to leave people, places, or things behind that do not serve us anymore. You must put one foot in front of the other and keep on going. One step at a time is a work in progress. Before you know it, you will have taken the giant steps you never thought you could take.

You may wonder how you hear this voice within. We all have the tools built in us that God put there to connect to Him. We connect to the spirit living in us. The spirit is in us the day we are born, residing within throughout our life. People will acknowledge this spirit living within as many things, as the Holy Spirit, spirit, universe, or God. I did accept the Holy Spirit into my life. When I accepted the Holy Spirit into my life, I felt a big change. I felt more in tune with the spirit living in me, and I could hear a lot clearer. But I found that it takes work to hear see and understand, and have confidence that what you are being shown is correct. I have had these inner connections my whole life, and I believe they are born in each one of us. Whatever you want to believe is your path right now. I am here to explain how we can hear and understand these inner workings, inner connections, and the voice within – how both of these inner and outer connections guide us in our daily living.

I hear the voice within speaking to me all the time. We need to learn how to hear this voice within and decipher that voice from all the chatter that goes on in our mind. You may wonder is this really possible? Yes, it is possible, but with all things you must take the time and do the work to really understand how it works.

I'm going to start with a dream I had. It was so amazing. I felt like I could stay there forever. I was in heaven in a classroom with God teaching me. He wanted me to teach people about the inner workings and inter connections between us, how people can connect to this and be guided in every area of their life. He was teaching me all of these things I'm going to share with you now. He told me not to worry about what people would think. People were getting off track, and He wanted us to be aware of the tools within us that lead, guide, and direct us every single day of our lives.

That day I got this message in my dream, I was bombarded with so much information about the inter connection and inner workings, it all just came together. I had been learning about this for years and how it worked but I wasn't teaching it. The dream was showing me just what I needed to do and how to teach it, and the dream was also showing me it was time to start teaching this. I was to start now, and in the small things I would be rewarded. I shouldn't look at small baby steps as worthless. I must take the first steps and do what He has been calling me to do.

I was receiving one thing after another, total confirmation that God wants His people to learn to connect to the spirit. He wants His people to connect completely to Him and to learn to trust the spirit that lives within. He wants you to trust in the abilities that He has put in you. He wants you to know we are all interconnected and there is so much more out there, and here on this earth, that has always been here to help us. You have the power within you to do more than you ever dreamed possible.

This dream was truly amazing. I knew it was straight from God and I really wanted to stay there forever. But He gave me a job to do and I know that this is my journey, my path and I needed to obey what He was showing me to do. Too many people have lost that connection with God and feel like He doesn't help us along the way. We may think maybe, just maybe, once in my lifetime, I will receive a miracle. That couldn't be further than the truth. I have had so many miracles in my life, I can't even begin to count. I'm sure each one of you have as well. I also believe and feel like He has given me many miracles I didn't even know about. Ones that may have saved me in my day-to-day life that I could not have known, because He took care of it before it even happened.

When you learn to listen and hear, you will wonder how you ever could have lived without this guidance. You will realize that you are guided every step of the way if you learn to tune into the source within. You will find that there is so much more to this guidance that is always with you.

There are many ways that God speaks to us, I will share them as I go along.

The first one I would like to talk about is intuition. We all have intuition. You can call it whatever you want. It is a tool in us from God and people have labeled it as intuition. We can say we have intuition, most of us accept it, but I feel we really don't understand intuition. Sometimes, I like to dissect a word. You hear a word but do you really and truly understand the word? This is something that is very important within us that we really don't seem to know how to home in on. When we learn to tune in and use this in the way God intended it for our lives, you will wonder why you took it for granted and didn't use it more often.

Some people will use it more than others, I'm not saying you don't use your intuition, I'm saying we need to learn to tune in more to our intuition. Once you learn to do this, it will change your life for the better. I'm going to dissect what intuition is through the definition. Since this is a big part of my book, learning to tune into your gifts, I'd like to give you the definition. This will help you better understand intuition. Intuition is one of these tools or gifts built in us. Once you read it you will find this will cover a number of ways that God

4

speaks to you. The definition is:

Intuition: The ability to understand something immediately, without the need for conscious reasoning.
Synonyms: Instinct, intuitiveness, sixth sense, clairvoyance, second sight.
A thing that one knows or considers likely from instinctive feelings, rather than conscious reasoning. Hunch, feeling, in one's bones, inkling, sneaking suspicion, idea, sense, gut feeling, gut instinct.
Ability to acquire knowledge without proof, or conscious reasoning or understanding how the knowledge was acquired.
Immediate apprehension or cognition without reasoning or inferring.
The power of faculty of gaining direct knowledge or cognition without evident rational thought and inference.
A knowing without knowing.
It's always there whether we know it or not.

Now you have a lot of insight to what intuition means, our inner hearing. The last line says, "it's always there whether we know it or not." This is why learning to acknowledge these inner workings and tune into them is key. It will help you make better decisions quicker and receive answers to your questions faster. You will be amazed you never knew how to use your intuition in this way.

How do we use intuition and learn to understand it better? There are several different ways intuition will show you things. One way is in an emergency; it may stir something inside of you that saves you from making a big mistake. It can save you from getting hurt or even save you from death.

This is a gift from God. A part of God living in us. Learning to connect to our intuition and trust it is such a wonderful gift. I am all about seeking God and I always knew He does so much more for us than we could ever imagine. When I seek and hear Him, sometimes I feel like I need to have Him confirm what I have heard, He will always show me again and again through lots of different ways. Sometimes He will send someone to speak to me. And if need be, He will lead me over and over again to someone or something until I finally wake up and get it.

Yes, there are times when I really need someone to help me. I have filled my mind with all kinds of ways to connect to God, yet not use any of them. Sometimes I can block or be misguided by the negative whispers that I haven't realized have drawn me away from my connection to God.

We may find that we are listening and we hear our intuition but we are not applying what we are being shown. I think that we all go through this, maybe a few times or maybe a lot of times, but we all go through this once in a while. I have done this. I have been shown things and I have written them down and seem to be blocked. Then someone comes into my path and helps me and guides me and shows me the very things I have written down. My intuition (God's guidance) was working all along but my mind was not applying what my intuition was showing me. How many times have we said I should have listened to that little voice telling me to do that?

There are many people who don't even realize that this exists. I'm here to tell you these are gifts from God put in each one of us. We can choose to use them or not. But these gifts are there. They are a part of our makeup. The more you learn what these gifts are and how to use them, the more amazed you'll find life to be. Trusting in your intuition means you are trusting in God to help you and show you what you need to do. Yes, God will show you the way, believe it, look for it and don't ever give up. He is always with us guiding us every step of the way, if you let him.

The more I learn about intuition, the more I realize that this is truly one of our connections to God. It's one of the names we have given the God within us. He never ceases to amaze me and show me more and more – I say that all the time but it's true! He directed me to Joseph Murphy talking about intuition and once again showed me just how important it is to use and listen to your intuition. When we learn to trust our intuition, we will go further than we ever thought possible. When we are spending time seeking God through quiet prayer and meditation, we will realize just how much He uses our intuition to commune with us.

I will say this a lot in this book God uses books to speak to me. I think that's why I love to have lots of books. I think it's harder to be directed to a digital book than to just go over to a book you are drawn to open and read. Maybe with this new age of computers and distractions, reading a book is becoming a lost art. Books may be your tool as well, or it may be something else. I am often guided to a book through strong feelings and my intuition, or someone will give me a book to read and it is just what I needed to hear. It is through my intuition that I know that this book is what I need at just that moment.

Before I go on, I would like to share this scripture in the Bible that says something that we should all look at closely and really try to understand. It is Matthew 13:13 -15 (NIV):

"Though seeing, they do not see; though hearing, they do not hear or understand. In them is fulfilled the prophecy of Isaiah: You will be ever hearing but never understanding; you will be ever seeing but never perceiving. For this people's heart has become calloused; they hardly hear with their ears, and they have closed their eyes. Otherwise they might see with their eyes, and hear with their ears, and understand with their hearts and turn, and I would heal them."

This is something that we need to understand: the importance of spending quiet time within. It will help you see hear and understand. It will help you stay on course and to not lose your way, because you have lost the ability to trust in what you are being shown through these gifts we all have within. It is time to start seeing, hearing, and understanding all the ways God communicates to us.

Here are a few ways that God speaks to us. I call some of these things my little voice or my screaming voice. Let's think about these things for a minute, how long have you had these inner workings in you? I know I have had these inner workings in me my whole entire life. I believe I was born with these inner workings, these tools to help lead, guide, and direct me.

There is a saying when the student is ready the teacher will appear. I am here to teach you how to tune into these tools within. You may be ready or maybe you're not. But I am here to share with you how to tune into your inner workings, that also lead, guide, and direct you in your life's journey. If you are ready, then you will receive.

I'd like to share with you a few stories from my life that will show you how promptings, voices, and gut feelings helped me. I have had many of these times, but I am just going to share three.

The first story, I was driving my little BMW on a highway. It was sleeting and hailing, there was about four inches of sleet and hail on the road. It was dreary, dark, and the sun was nowhere to be found. I was driving rather fast for the road conditions but I was headed down south and I wanted out of this weather. I wasn't driving over the speed limit, but much too fast for the road conditions. Why and how I was driving so fast and getting away with it, I don't really know. I saw people passing me by and I was shocked they too were driving even faster than I was in the bad weather.

All of a sudden, I heard this still small voice telling me to get off the road and clear my windshield. I really didn't want to listen but I kept hearing it. After a while, I said God could you bring out the sun to clear off my windshield. To my amazement, the sun came out for only about a minute. It helped the windshield only slightly. Again, the voice was back telling me to get off the road and clear off my windshield. That voice was quiet and relentless until finally I obeyed.

I got off the exit fast, it only took a few minutes to clean off the windshield and wipers and get quickly back on the highway. Only to come to a complete stop. After a little while of sitting there I turned on the radio to see what was up, it said there was a wreck with trucks on top of cars. It was going to take about six hours to clear. For some reason I left space in between the cars in front of me, I got out and told people we were going to be here for about six hours and started telling people if we turned around and took the shoulder a couple hundred feet back we could go on the turn around and get off the highway. So that's what a lot of us did. That space in front of me helped to get some of us turned around. They detoured us around the wreck, which took us right next to the highway and where I could see it. Guess what I saw, all those cars and trucks that were passing me were in that wreck. I knew I was saved from that awful wreck.

The next story I would like to share with you, is the screaming voice in my head. I was hanging flower plants on my porch and this screaming voice in my head was telling me to go get a step ladder. My screaming voice was telling me to stop standing on unsafe things to hang the flower pots. It was telling me to go get my brand-new ladder my husband just bought me and use it. I ignored that screaming voice, each plant I put up, that voice kept screaming in my head to stop. But I refused to listen. Hanging the last flower basket with that voice still screaming in my head, I fell off the chair I was standing on, I heard a loud crack. I lay there and knew I broke a bone in my foot. I was laid up for six months with no weight bearing on my foot. The doctor decided to let it heal naturally so I didn't have to have a pin in it. Had I listened to that screaming voice; I wouldn't have had to deal with that incident.

The last of these stories I will share is when something came over me. I was in my car coming home from my daughter's house and I decided I wanted to turn down another road to get to my house. I rarely use this road to get to my house, but for some reason I wanted to this time. All of a sudden something came over me and I couldn't turn the wheel. In that split second a huge semi-truck turned into the middle turn lane, driving rather fast. Had I turned, we would have hit head on and I would have been killed.

These three stories, different promptings and different endings to the story. This is why learning to listen to these promptings, voices, or feelings can, and do save you from bad things happening to you. We all have them. They are built into our whole being. We must learn to hear them, tune in to them, trust them, and do what they are telling us to do.

We can learn to tune in daily to hear answers to simple things as well. We are always asking questions that need answers. Sometimes we get the answers and sometimes we don't. It's not because the answer isn't there, we are just not hearing it. We think we don't hear the answer. Sometimes the answer may come in promptings to do something for you to receive your answer. These solutions, ideas, and promptings are built into our makeup. I call them the voice within.

Maybe you have something that keeps coming up all the time that you must do and you are not doing it. If it keeps coming back to you over and over, then it is something you need to address and something you probably need to do. You may not know how to do it, or maybe you don't want to do it so you make excuses. Maybe you want to do it, deep down in your heart, but you just can't bring yourself to do it.

If you are having a hard time with this feeling, keep asking for guidance so you will be able to do what you know deep down you must do. I have had things I know I should do and haven't done for years. It has been a big hindrance for me to move forward. It's kind of like getting up on a huge cliff and jumping into the water. You get up on that rock and stand there and stand there, afraid to jump off. You may keep walking away from it, only to come back and try again and again, until one day you take the leap and wonder why you waited so long. Why did you let fear stop you from taking that leap? You found it was easier than you made it out to be. Most of the time that little voice you hear is correct. It's that tiny second voice, that second guessing one, that says, "I'm not sure, I'm afraid, it will never work" that keeps us from moving forward and doing what we should be doing.

You will know when you are doing something that is not right, you will feel it and you will not be able to deny these feelings. Every part of you will be saying this is wrong. Don't ignore that feeling or thought.

There are things I know I need to do but have not taken the leap of faith because I feel I don't know how. I don't know how to let go and trust. But each day, I let go more and more of my life to trusting in doing the things I'm shown to do. Learning to trust in yourself is not easy, but when you put the time in to seek and hear, you will find the right way to go. If at times you feel unsure of what you are hearing, just keep seeking and you will continue to receive answers. Until you finally acknowledge and believe that the answers you are hearing are exactly what you need. Then start doing what your inner guidance is showing you to do.

The answers can and do come from many different places and in different ways. When I draw close to God through prayer and meditation, and spend quiet time in this universe I receive. Taking walks in the woods or near the river or streams brings me closer to hear and feel Him. Just enjoying the beauty in nature, letting go of all the noise and chatter draws me closer to my source of renewal. This recharges me and I find I receive so many answers and I feel so much better. I feel refreshed and renewed, ready to take on the world once again.

On these next pages I will show you two great exercises to help you hear the voice within connecting to the universe. In these examples I give you don't try to use my meanings or anyone else's meaning. This works because it has to do with your thoughts and your meanings. Your inner workings telling you what you need to know. This is just an example of how my inner workings see things.

These are exercises you should do often to connect you and help you hear, and help you find answers you need throughout your life. They should become a part of your daily life.

Hearing the universe speaking through a walk

Exercise to help you hear what the Universe is showing you

The Universe speaks to you all the time, trying to help guide you and show you the way. When we learn to tune in to the signs all around us, we will be able to connect to these signs and understand what they are saying. This is a simple exercise that will open your eyes to a better understanding to your connections to your source within and all around us

Take a walk with a pen and pad and write down what your eyes are drawn to. Or what you may feel such as an itch on your ear or eye, or a color or song you think of. I keep myself focused on taking my walk. While I walk, I just enjoy walking and being quiet and allow my mind to go where it naturally goes. I don't try to force what I see. Don't overthink it. Just walk and when you see your eyes go to something write it down. Write to the bottom of the page and then stop. You can stop and sit and look at what you have written or go inside to sit and write.

Look at each thing you have written and think about what each one means to you. For instance, a stop sign means stop or a fire truck may mean fire, but the color red could be your favorite color. We all have a different thought that comes to us when we look at something. When you look at the word you have written think about what it means to you. Don't overthink it. Just try to go with what it means to you at this time. First impressions are probably correct, but not always, it may need a little more. You can make this simple or hard. DON'T OVERTHINK THIS.

Take each word and write across from the word what you feel it is saying to you. What you feel that word or words mean. When you get to the bottom go back and read it through the best you can. Once you start doing this it will get easier and easier. I can make a whole message from doing this. You will find that everything around you is speaking to you. Communicating with you helping you with answers you need to know.

This side of page write down what you see - then to the right, add a little line to connect the word with what you feel is the meaning of the word at this time.

Example

A clear mud puddle	I can see clearly
Stop sign	I need to stop and look
Itchy eye	Look
Someone opening a door	A door of opportunity is opening for me

When we go back and read what we have written it may look like this. "I can see clearly and I really need to stop and look, really take a good look and see that a door is being opened for me right now. I really have to pay attention to see.

When you learn to work with this, you will find that it gives you answers you need, help from within and from all around you, the Universe. And it will get easy and you will be able to do it really fast.

Sitting quietly to hear the universe

You can do this exercise sitting quietly, while you close your eyes, or keep them open, or both. I find when I do this exercise this way, I may notice more itches. I may get an itch near my eye, which for me it's telling me to look or I'll get an itch on my ear that tells me to listen. For you, it may mean something else, like how the itch was annoying to you. You need to feel what the meaning really means to you. At first, an itch may seem annoying and that may be what it is saying at that time, but with practice you may find it is telling you something different. It takes time to tune in and focus on things around you or things you hear or feel. It is in learning to be quiet, tuning into what is all around you, and noticing the things that are trying to get your attention that you'll find the answers you need. We have so much noise and distraction in our lives, especially in this new world of electronics. We don't realize that the art of being quiet has become almost extinct. It is in the quiet we find answers. We find what we need.

This exercise is the same exercise as taking a walk, but instead of walking you are sitting. As you sit, figure out what you are drawn to and what these things mean to you. For me, I have to work out the meaning as soon as I am done looking, because the answers may not come to me the same way they were intended to later on. You should do this exercise from start to finish without being distracted.

This exercise is to sit quietly and notice what the Universe is drawing your thoughts, hearing, and eyes to. Tune into yourself and what is speaking all around to find your answers.

Start this exercise by sitting someplace quiet, in a room in your house with no distractions. You can go outside or go sit in a park or on a bench somewhere. When you are ready to begin, relax your mind and start breathing in and out. You can count your breaths quietly in and out, or however you feel to quiet your mind from the chatter in your thoughts, calming your mind from any distractions. By breathing and keeping your thoughts on your breath, it will help you to keep negative chatter out. Get yourself relaxed by simply breathing in and out however you choose. You can breathe in, hold a second, then breathe out until you calm yourself and your mind. Sitting quietly, you can close your eyes, keep them open, or move between both. Whatever you do, keep still and focus on what you hear, see, or feel.

Everything matters, even if you have an itchy nose or hand, or if you hear a noise of any kind. Try to keep your mind free of any chatter. You are just feeling and acknowledging the things around you drawing your attention. If a color pops up, a song, a number write it down. Just make sure you keep your mind free from chatter by keeping your focus on breathing. If you are sitting outside watching the activity all around you, notice where your eyes are drawn to and write it down. When you've gotten to the end of the page and you feel ready to stop, then do so.

Now go back and look at each thing you have written down. What does it mean to you? Don't try to think too much, it's best to go with your first answer. Each person has a different meaning of what that thing they wrote down means. You can write the answer on another page but while you're writing, keep it next to the words you wrote. You will find that everything has a meaning and is telling you something.

You will find that what you look at is speaking to you helping you through life by giving you the messages you need.

Write on the left side what   Write on the right side what
      you are drawn to   the words mean to you

Once you have written the meaning of each thing you were drawn to put the sentences together and you will have a message from the Universe. This is a quiet way God will speak and guide you through life.

A message in a strange way

I'd like to share a story about this really annoying bird. I am always asking God to speak to me, sometimes over and over again. God is always gracious to answer. I had a season when every time I went outside on the side porch to work or eat my lunch, this bird would squawk and it would not stop. It always squawked the same note over and over again. It seemed like it would never ever stop. It would annoy me without end. It stressed me out, it took away my peace. I wouldn't be able to concentrate or function. I didn't see any bird's nest nearby that I was disturbing either. I would give up and go inside.

One day, I realized that annoying bird was telling me something. There were several messages I got out of it. One of the messages was, I was that squawking bird, I was always squawking to God over and over about the same things, but I wasn't doing what He was telling me or showing me to do. The second part I got out of it was God is squawking the answers over and over to me but I am refusing to do what he is telling me to do. I would think "Oh yeah, right, God I get it - I hear you, God." Then the next day I would get up and forget what I was shown and continue to squawk to God. Sometimes, I would try to do what He was leading me to do, and if it didn't work out as fast as I wanted it to, I would give up and go back to squawking.

When I heard this in real life from that bird, it was so annoying I couldn't stand it. I would retreat. I did not want to acknowledge the message that I was getting from God. Can you imagine how God feels? We need to really examine our lives. God gives us all kinds of messages in all kinds of ways, but since we are not taking the time to hear God, we are missing the answers most of the time. By the way, once I got the message, the bird miraculously stopped squawking.

I want to stress to you in a good way that God will speak to you in all kinds of ways if you just open yourself up to Him. Stop worrying what people say, you need to follow your heart. This is your journey, your life. I have learned to do this and I am so much more at peace than I used to be. Connecting to the God source that lives in you is what we are all searching for throughout life. People search their whole lives for what will make them happy. They will look everywhere to find happiness and peace. They will go to a number of people asking for someone to please show them the answers they need. They will ask, please can you help me find out what is wrong with me. We have to realize we are not connecting to the God source living within us. When we plug into the source, we will get charged and we will have the energy to do what it takes for us to have a better life. It's not in a pill, a church, a psychologist, a reader, or a doctor. It lives within us. It is God and with this connection we will find that peace and feel contentment. Again, it is in the quietness that we will find what we are looking for.

We may think we have God (our source of connection) in our lives because we feel we are doing the right things, we say our prayers, and we do good deeds for others. These are all good things to do. But if you are still not feeling the way you want to feel, then you need to take an honest look at your life. Are you really connected to God the way you should be, that source inside of you, that guides you? Do you hear and feel things all around you that are answering your questions, your cries? Do you feel that God is speaking to you all the time? Or do you feel that God is silent?

God is here for us; He hears us when we speak. He is trying to communicate to us daily. Sometimes, it's in a simple way and sometimes it is in a huge way. He will speak to you if you open up to Him and learn how He is communicating to you. Many of us have seen Him help us in simple ways and some have seen Him help them in big ways. I want you to realize that He is with you in the small stuff and the big stuff, if you learn to hear, see, and feel the ways He answers you. He works within you and guides you every single day.

Now let's talk about another way God (source) will speak to you. We've talked about intuition, now let's talk about our subconscious mind. This is another inner connection that God uses to speak to us. We are led using these inner connections. I'm going to talk about knowing. Using these three gifts in combination will bring you into a deeper connection to the voice within. They will help unlock answers you seek.

I'll share a little story how God gave me a sign that I was going in the right direction. I was meditating on intuition and subconscious together. I wanted to work on the two and write about them and teach them together. I had already written the pages and was ready to teach them. I walked into this store and was led to look at a rock. The placard on the rock said that it was for intuition and subconscious. To me it was a synchronicity, a sign, my answer. Simple confirmations like these happen all the time and we can miss them. It never ceases to amaze me and I never grow tired of this. I will never take it for granted. When you start acknowledging these different signs, you will wonder how you could have missed them.

This is just a simple little thing God used. Now that I have learned to use these tools within, I see that He shows us things like this all the time. I ask questions all the time, I am open to receiving the answers and I can recognize the answers that come. I now carry a question and answer book around with me all the time. I have found over the years that I will ask a question, I will receive the answer, and somehow, I forget the answer. I love to journal and I write everything in my journaling book. I found that it is very hard to go back over my journaling for answers to my questions. I find that all I have to do is look in my question answer book and I can see it clearly; I don't forget and it is so much easier to keep track of. I never leave home without my little book.

I have found that I will get flash thoughts popping into my head all day long, things like answers, an idea, or a solution to something I need. It comes in and goes out of your head so fast that it is easy to lose that thought. If you want to stay more in tune and on top of things, I suggest you get a little notebook and carry it with you. You will be surprised at all the answers you receive throughout the day. They are valuable gifts we tend to lose because we don't acknowledge them when we receive them. So be sure and write them down. Once you start doing this you will realize how many times you get answers to questions you asked, and don't even know it. One thing I call these things is synchronicities. When you receive one, you might say, "Wow, that is my answer!", or your jaw will drop because you realized you received the answer to what you needed. Whatever you call them or say when you get your answer, try not to forget them.

Here is another interesting thing that just happened to me after I wrote this last paragraph, I looked at my watch and I saw 11:11. Sometimes, God speaks to me through numbers. This one comes up all the time. But when I am in a place where I am really needing God to reassure me He is with me and I'm not alone, He will send me a sign. One kind of sign He sends me is double, triple, and quadruple numbers. Numbers seem to bombard me; they are everywhere I turn. As I've said there are many ways God speaks to me, and how He speaks to others may be different. Some people may find pennies everywhere. As I've said before I will feel led to a book open it up and there is the answer I need. I'm led to books in the strangest ways. One time, I was in the woods and someone gave me a book they had written. It was amazing and spoke to me in high volumes (and it still does when I think about it.)

Another way I get confirmations to situations is seeing an eagle. There have been a number of times I have been thinking about a situation and what I should do about it, I may have the answer but am still rolling it around in my mind, and I will see an eagle at that exact moment. This has happened enough times to me that it isn't just a coincidence.

I used to see the eagles a lot in the job I had, where I would drive up and down the river. Just when I needed an answer, I would see an eagle - just at the right time. Once, I stopped that job, I didn't see eagles very often. Much to my surprise, eagles built a nest in my back yard along the mountain. I had a koi pond and that was very concerning to me. I didn't want them there. The eagles that I loved so much became something I was afraid of. However, they were bringing with them a message. When you really look closely at things, there is a message you can learn from just about anything.

As I said I was concerned they were going to eat my fish. I told my husband we needed to do something before they ate our fish. He said he would but it would take some time to complete. One day, there were two eagles circling around over my head in front of the fish pond. All of a sudden, the message came loud and clear: I needed to stop waiting for other people and take charge of the situation. If I didn't do something, the fish were going to be eaten. I covered up the pond with what I could to deter them from getting into the pond. I told my husband I was going to get a net and put it over the pond to save the fish. The next day, he built frames for the net and the fish have been safe ever since. Had I waited and not listened to the message I received; I would have been very sad. The message was also telling me to stop waiting for other people to do the things I wanted done, because I can make them happen. Stop procrastinating. Do the things you want done, find a way and make it happen.

It may seem strange that God speaks to me through birds. Sometimes birds would fly in front of my path for miles and miles. Sometimes this would happen for days and days in a row. I started asking other people if this has ever happened to them. I found that very few people have ever experienced this. I thought it was just a coincidence, but I found that this was not the case. It seemed that when I needed to feel I wasn't alone, or I needed to be guided in a tough situation those birds would be there, like angels flying all around me. This would help me feel like it was going to be okay, I was not alone, I am on the right path, stay strong. There are so many signs we miss because we shut out the ways God speaks to us. Think about it the next time something out of the ordinary happens to you. Learning that you are being spoken to through unusual ways will amaze you. It will help you see that you are never alone and the universe is there guiding you all the time. He speaks through many ways and will give you many signs, until finally you get the message. Wouldn't it be great to learn how to get the message sooner and faster? Yes, it is possible.

Your subconscious mind

Let's get back to talking about the subconscious mind. There are a lot of good books available teaching you about the subconscious mind. I like Joseph Murphy's books. These books will help you to use your subconscious mind to help you reprogram your thinking so you will draw what you want to you. These gifts or tools within, as I call them, I don't think we understand exactly how we can use them to help us in our day to day lives. We may think we do but learning to really apply positive programming into our subconscious mind is something we overlook.

I would like to give you a simple phrase we all have read or heard a million times, "You become what you think about all day long" by Ralph Waldo Emerson, yet I think it goes in one ear and out the other. We love this phrase, but do we really apply it?

Let's look at this simple phrase. Do you think about what is wrong with you all day long, or what you should be doing all day long? How about your weight? Or how bad, unhappy, or mad you are? Or how life is unfair to you? Or you allow everything that happens to you to become your life. You think it will never get better and you find it doesn't get better and the same things are happening to you over and over again. You continue to confess; why does this always happen to me. It's just who I am. I am what I am. I just can't change. Boohoo is me. Or, you have so much drama in your life. You can't figure it out. You're not happy about it, so you just feel you have to live with it.

I'm here to tell you, you can change it. But only if you really want to change it. Most of the time we don't even realize that

25

we allow our lives to be this way. We'll say this is just the way it is. You unconsciously do these things and more of this comes back to you. Some people call this the law of attraction.

If you asked anyone who knew you, they could tell you what you need to do. They could tell you what you do and how you could change things. You don't realize you follow the same patterns that give you the same results every time and you continue with these patterns that keep you stuck. Most of the time these people won't tell you because they don't want to hurt your feelings. You may not want to continue to be friends with them if they told you. You really want your friends to sympathize with you. If they would tell you what they really see, it would make you mad or you would excuse it away by saying things like, "That can't be right, they don't know what they're talking about."

We all have these tendencies – so how do we change this? First, try and catch yourself every time you go off on anything that is negative, especially against yourself. Remember these old sayings, "If you think you can't, you won't. If you think bad things will happen to you, they will. If you think you're not good enough, then you won't be good enough." It's all what you think of yourself. Just do it, make the thought changes in your thinking. If you think bad of yourself all the time, you will believe it and more of this will come back to you.

This is the time to draw near to God in quiet time and ask how to resolve this pattern. Spend quiet time after you have asked the question and, when you are through with quiet time, take your pad and pen and start writing. You will find the answers will flow to you and you will also get all kinds of synchronicities or confirmations to your questions. If you find you didn't get an answer right away, then stay open and the answers will come to you in all kinds of ways; people can say just what you need to hear, you'll read something, or you'll hear something. Stay open to hear the answers come to you. Write them down and realize if you change these things, you will overcome and handle life better than you did before. These old patterns or habits will die off and you will become a new person.

There are many quotes out there that will help you. I could write all kinds of quotes to help you, but these quotes and sayings written to help us are just words. Until we allow them to sink inside of our thinking, our subconscious, etching them into our whole being, to really change our thoughts about who we are, they will only be words, just plain old words. We must do all we can do to make these words soak deep inside of us, like a dry sponge soaking up water. We must fill it up with the things we desire and we must make every inch of our mind, body, and spirit believe this to be true.

Faith, trust and belief; we feel we need to achieve our dreams. We do this by filling our thinking with what we need, what we want, and what has to change. It is our thinking that needs to change. Thinking is everything in our bodies. It controls everything. From our attitude, to how we see things, even manifesting in our health.

How can we start to change our thinking? We need to start programming our thoughts with what it is we want our lives to be. In Joseph Murphy's books, he talks about sitting quietly, saying a script you have written, and visualize it as already done. You can do this when you wake up in the morning, during the day, and before you go to bed. Getting into a sleepy, drowsy state is the best place to put things in your subconscious mind.

You have to get these thoughts deep down into your thinking so this will happen. When we say our mantra three or more times a day, we have to then start to visualize it continually believing that what we are saying is coming to pass. We have to guard our thoughts and keep the negative whispers out of our thoughts. This negative thinking or negative speaking can cancel out the work we are doing, speaking, and visualizing. You have to get all negative doubt out of your thinking so it allows the positive work to take hold and become reality. You have to fake it till you make it. If you can't do that, then start to visualize yourself receiving what you want. Picture how you would feel, then start feeling it as you receive it. Let all of your senses get into your vision. Make that dream so real, and it will become a reality. A dream is just a dream unless you make it real.

You may ask, "is it hopeless?" No, it isn't if you are willing to go the extra mile to change your life and have the things you want or to be the person you want to become. You must do the work. It isn't a free lunch, it takes work, and if you put the work into having what you want, you will receive it. There is a statistic that says only about five percent of people will do the work needed to succeed after going to a self-help function or reading a great self-help book and really put what they learn into practice. Don't let that be you. Make the decision to do the work. Stop just dreaming and start making that dream become a reality.

I have lots of positive sayings I have collected. If it's, out their chances are I have it. I have positive phrases all over my house. I have writings all over of positive uplifting phrases. If I don't allow it to take hold and get inside of me, so it takes deep root way down deep inside of me in my subconscious thinking, then

I will find that it will never ever work and I will never ever change.

Here's a simple example, something I used to say about myself: I just can't type -- I just can't get it. There's just no way. I took a typing class. I even went out and bought a voice-to-text typing program. I tried that and found I would have to go back and re-write things. Long story short, I learned to type, I like it now and I no longer am afraid to type. I just kept doing it and I stopped the negative talk about it and I didn't give up.

You must get your desire deep on the inside to let that desire become a belief that takes over, and then that belief will take you to the next step. Use your subconscious mind. Start doing what you can to program your mind positively toward all you want to change about you and your life. And most importantly, "Stop telling yourself how bad you are."

I suggest writing down a positive message, find the time -- no, make the time, to say it at least three times a day. Read this phrase with feeling and believe that it will come to pass. If any negative comes in, call it a liar and replace those lies with a positive suggestion. Remember everything about our lives is in our own thinking, it's what we believe. We are creating what we believe, what we think we are. That thinking can be changed if we believe we can change it. Keep the naysayers away from you, especially your own thoughts if they are trying to be a naysayer. Replace the naysayers with, "Yes, I can and I will!" I have changed my words from "I can" or "I will" to "I manifest", and I added to it "I have the favor." Repeat your positive statement as many times as needed. And NEVER EVER GIVE UP!

You can write out a positive message of the things you want to change in your life. Make sure it is exactly what you want for your life. Use your phone and download a voice recorder app and record a soothing positive message slowly. Listen to it three times a day. Put it on so it keeps playing over again. Especially at night before bed and let your voice lull you to sleep. There are a number of messages on YouTube you can listen to. There are many good messages out there. We have many hours of negative talk pouring into our minds, that's why we have to make the time to feed and water positive thought as much as we can, wherever we can. I have my phone by my bed. I listen to the messages I made before bed and I plug them in before I get out of bed in the morning.

Use your subconscious mind to help you reprogram your thinking. Remember, your subconscious doesn't know if it's true or false, it believes what it hears. If it is always hearing how bad things are, it will believe that's the way it is. Your subconscious mind is a powerful tool that you can use to help you become who you want to be, and what you want to have or what you want to do.

Let's take a good look at your subconscious and your conscious mind. They need to get on the same page, in agreement with each other. Working on one will help the other, by feeding your mind positive thoughts, and avoiding negative talk. It all takes work, but it all starts with one step at a time. Start building yourself up every day, all day long. You must get that negative thinking about yourself out of your everyday life. Working on your subconscious, through feeding it the things you need and want are important. Spend time feeling what you are saying, visualize your outcome. Go to sleep and wake up to a positive message that will feed your subconscious thinking and make such a difference. This helps to bring your conscious thinking in tune with your subconscious. When they are in agreement, all will come together. Getting these two in tune and on the same page in agreement is key to receiving what you desire. When you have this constant tug of war, you will always be in conflict trying to make things work. Learn to get your entire thinking on the same page and in the place, you want to be. Once you do that, watch what happens. You will find that you will receive the answers you desire, things will change, and your life will be what you want.

Desire

You need to get your desire straight. This is incredibly important. You must really think about your desire -- really take a long, hard look at it and make sure it is truly what you want. I found that sometimes what I thought I really wanted, when taking a hard look at it, was not what I wanted at all. Make sure in your mind you are certain you really want it. When you think about your desire, listen to what comes back to you. The voice within will give you all you need, so make sure it's what you want. I have found that sometimes to receive what I wanted I had to go through some rough patches. At times, I didn't get it and was so glad I didn't, because I really didn't want it. If you learn to always work with the voice within, your source, the God within, you will receive all the answers you need.

A good way to find out what you really want is to write. I start writing what I want. Underneath I will write the pros and cons for each thing I have written down. I also write what I am thinking about for each thing I have on my list. You will find that this is a really good way to hear things, through working with your thoughts using a pen and paper. You will be able to go back and look at what you wrote, add things, and really be able to see if this is truly what you want. You may find that the cons are stopping you from receiving what you want. Unconsciously, you may have negative thoughts about having what you think you want. It is important to work out the kinks so what you want will come to you. Maybe you may find that you really don't want what you thought you wanted. Do the work to receive the right things you want for your life. Stop procrastinating and get that work done so you receive the desires of your heart. While you do this work, you can ask what is needed to be done to help you acquire your dreams.

Remember, when you connect and put effort into things, they will get done.

I want to continue with more gifts that are in our subconscious mind and this is our next topic to talk about.

Precognition

Definition: foreknowledge of an event, especially foreknowledge of a paranormal kind.

People feel precognition is something to fear. Here's the thing, your mind is telling you things every minute. But most of the time, we find it all a confusing mess of chatter. We want to stop all the chatter because we don't know how to decipher what the chatter is telling us. We sometimes don't know how to get away from it to quiet our minds.

There are a lot of things written about precognition. I believe that there are people out there that are born with these natural abilities that know things in advance what will happen. There are all different names for people with this gift.

I had a very interesting experience when I thought that I was finished writing this workbook. I felt led to precognition. I always look things up so I have a better understanding, along with much seeking quietly for right answers. I was feeling a little apprehensive about it after reading some of the things on this topic. There are some people that home in on this gift of being able to see into the future to help people and make a living using this gift. That is their path, not mine. I am not about that at all. I know what I have been directed to write and teach. What I've been shown are ways to tune into these things within us that will help better our lives and hear the voice within that will lead us and guide us. I won't go into detail about how I was directed, and how my questions got answered because it would take many more pages. I want you to know that I did a lot of research and spent a lot of quiet time when I was led to this to make sure I wasn't off track. Someone handed me a book on precognition. I opened this book and the first page my eyes saw answers to my questions and was total confirmation that I was on track. As always, my jaw drops when the answers come in ways I could not have made up. I can't remember the name of the book that confirmed my research, sorry to say. It was totally right on.

You will find that when you learn to sort through what all the chatter is trying to tell you and use it to your advantage; you'll be so much more at peace. We have the answers within us. We actually know the answers, unfortunately, we sometimes refuse to take heed of the answers. When I really look at something, I need an answer to and I do the work, I will receive it. Most times, I've known the answer all along. It's just that I don't really want to accept it. That's the reason we block. We don't really want to hear the answer. We don't want to do the work, and we'll block it so we don't have to deal with it. Like exercise, we all know that we would feel so much better if we did it but we block it by saying we don't feel like it. We'll make every excuse there is to avoid it. Our bodies start feeling worse each day, and we'll go to the doctor for help. They tell us to get exercise, but we'd rather take the pill instead of doing the exercise. The doctor has to prescribe therapy because we won't do it on our own.

Once again, where is precognition? In our thinking. It's all about our thinking, our thoughts, in our brain, our mind. I will keep saying this over and over because this is what you need to learn. It is such a wonderful tool that God has put into our being that we just don't use to our advantage. We don't understand it, so we choose to ignore it, while others have it and have learned to use it more, and still others just have that natural ability born in them. Whatever amount you feel you have use it to help you. If you feel or sense something is going to happen, take heed to it. When I get those feelings, I will follow them, even if they don't make sense to me. If I feel like I shouldn't do something and it won't leave me, then I don't do it. There is a reason we get these feelings. It is better to be safe than sorry.

The precognition feelings I am referring to are the 60 to 70% which come in dreams or vivid waking visions, flashing thoughts in the mind, and a sense of knowledge. It hits you and you can't shake the feeling. We all have this inner connection called precognition. When we learn to tune in and better understand our voice within, source, spirit, or God within, our precognition will become easier to understand as well. Once you learn to take the time to be still and draw inward to your source, you'll be more in tune with what the Universe, the angels, and the signs are showing you. These signs are sent to us all the time. You shouldn't be afraid of this gift, instead you should embrace it. Precognition is a part of the gifts we are born with. If we are a spiritual being born into a human body, then why should we fear spiritual ways God works to get our attention. We have so much more than we can ever imagine inside of us waiting to be tapped into. Again, I repeat, "Don't fear it, embrace it" and learn to go deeper so you will be able to know all the things you need to know, to have a better life. More connected and in control, knowing you have a source bigger than anything, here to help you in any way you need help and guidance. It takes a little time as in anything we want to do, but when you start you will find that it becomes a part of who you are and it will become second nature.

Some people have said that they have had feelings not to go on a plane and they choose to follow the feeling and the plane crashed. They will get this feeling come over them, or have a strong dream that sticks with them. These are all signs to help us in life. There are many people who have stories just like this and have followed their inner feelings. I have had them lots of times. But there is a difference in feeling afraid to do something like get on a plane because they are totally afraid to fly. Fear and knowing are two different things. One says I know that I know, the other says I am afraid and fear will not leave. You just sense it is different with a knowing. You may never know the reason this premonition came over you. It might not be in a plane crash; it might be in something like the car ride to the airport or someone you love may get sick or hurt and need you immediately. You could have been in the wrong place at the wrong time and something bad would have happened. Once you become more in tune with your gifts it will help you decipher your feelings faster and more accurately. But again, we can still make mistakes because we don't follow what we are being shown. The more work we put in to quiet time and seeking the more we will find control in our lives.

The more I live my life like this the more I will trust and follow my inner connection. I will stop blocking, ignoring, or try to do it my way instead of the way my inner connection is leading me. I'm glad I am on this path to continue to learn to do the right thing and spend the quiet time I need with my source. I get better and better every day. ☺

While I was re-reading and changing things on this topic, something happened that I feel I need to share. Because it is another confirmation that God wanted me to know I am doing what He wants me to do, by adding this precognition. I was thinking I wanted to take my work by the river. But I had this feeling come over me don't go to the river, it's going to rain, so I sat on my covered back porch to work instead. The sun was out it was hot and the skies were beautiful blue with white puffy clouds. No rain for today and none in the forecast. I was working for about an hour and out of nowhere it started to rain.

Still sunny, still blue skies and white puffy clouds. I love to get these little things that tell me you're right on.

I want to share with you some exercises that I do to help me hear and see signs from God, our source. Once you learn how to do these exercises, you will find it will open the door for you to see how the Universe is used to give you messages in unusual ways. These messages will help you or be the answer you need. I don't know how long I used to say wow that was weird, when I would see these strange messages sent in a way, I know I would have missed before. Now I say that was amazing.

You may think that this way of connecting is work. To me it was changing myself to receive what I have been searching for my whole life. To be connected and to be able to have the things I want in life. To be secure that I am not alone and I have a power living in me I never realized was so powerful. I'm learning I can fit these changes into my life. Being connected. has made me much happier and more in control of my mind, body, and spirit. I still have all the time I need to do the things I love and need to do. Plus, I am getting rid of things that do not serve me anymore, things that are a big waste of time. I also found I wasted a lot of time sitting around being bored or unhappy, unmotivated or complaining about life. Once you get connected you will find things will change for the better. I feel calm and more at peace with who I am.

So, let's get to these great exercises

1. Before sleep

Before you go to sleep is the best time to ask questions. While you sleep, you will receive answers – while your conscious mind isn't interfering with your subconscious mind.

When I am ready to close my eyes and sleep for the night, I will ask a question. I will ask that the answer come to me and I expect it to come. I leave it with my mind and believe God will give me the answer I asked for. I let it go and then go to sleep. Keep a pen and pad on your night stand and grab it when you wake up in the morning and start writing. You should always keep a pad and pen handy, to write dreams, flash thoughts, or ideas. That is why they are called flashes, because they come in a flash and leave just as quickly.

Now just start writing. Don't worry about what you are writing. Sometimes you will wake up and have nothing to write about. Just write, if you say I feel tired and I want to sleep more, just write it, and write whatever comes into your head. I find I may start off not feeling like I have an answer, but after a little while things start pouring out. I will also write throughout the day. I find even making my breakfast a wealth of knowledge will be shown to me. You will find later that the things you need to be doing and the answers you need will be in those pages. If you are putting the time into doing this work, you will get your answers. With answers there is work that has to be put forth for your desires to come to pass. Learn to do this work and see what happens.

There is so much information out there on these topics,

precognition, intuition, your subconscious mind, and knowing. All of this is built into us as humans. It's our inner connections, the ability to know the answers and be guided. We will live a better life if we just learn to use these tools the way they were intended to be used. I don't believe for one moment we were to go through life not knowing how to connect to these God given gifts. These gifts will lead, guide and direct you if you just take the time and tune in. This will really give you a better way of life. Getting the answers to all our questions.

2. Lost item that needs to be found

When I have lost something and I can't seem to find it, I will stop and take a few deep breaths close my eyes ask where the item is, and then I will just focus on the thing I need to find. I do my best to keep out any distraction. I focus on the item and my breathing, until I feel released to move on. I then start to look for it, thoughts will pop into my head and most of the time I find it. There are times when I have to stop and quiet my mind and ask again. I'd say I find it about 98 percent of the time. Sometimes, I feel it is gone and I have to let it go.

3. Positive programming your subconscious mind

There are a lot of books that teach you about getting into a sleepy drowsy state to receive answers to questions you ask. Or to put a statement into your thinking so your mind will absorb it and help make it come to pass. As I've stated, I like Joseph Murphy's way of stilling your mind to hear. We have to look at our makeup, everything we say and do comes from our thinking. Everything! So why do we not realize that our brain is a very powerful tool, that we can use to help us achieve what we want. Through positive programming. Some people use this programming in a negative way. They call that brain washing.

We wonder why or how this can happen, you can take someone and brain wash them to do awful things. You have to realize we are what we hear and have programmed into our thinking. Good, bad or otherwise.

This is why we think differently. Why we believe what we believe. What we are hearing is who we become. That is the reason we have different religions, different cultures. Some people are nice, mean, happy, sad, depressed. It is what we allow into our thinking. We can change that by constantly programming our thoughts as to how and what we want to be, have, or become. It's all up to you. It's about taking the time and doing the work to change the way your mind thinks. It will change the way you look at life. It will help you let go of old habits and patterns, and draw to you the things you want.

Whatever you allow into your thoughts, all the time, is what you believe, and receive. It's that simple, so why not take this beautiful mind and use it for your good? Take the time to stop and get in this quiet drowsy state and repeat a positive statement, (you are planting the seed) then do this several times a day (you are watering and nourishing this seed.) Then, throughout the day keep watering that thought by repeating it. Repetition sinks it deep inside of you to help you believe and receive. Make sure you feel it and visualize that planted thought. Do this and don't give up, and keep kicking out that negative thinking. Kick out those bad habits or patterns that steal your positive changed thought. When you do this, you will find you will change, and that positive idea you've planted will grow and come into your life. Just don't worry about the how. It is only necessary to plant the seed, water and nourish it. Just don't miss the way it will happen. Keep your mind open to all kinds of possibilities. They may come in a way you are not familiar with. It may be a bit harder to do it differently then you thought it would be. Just continue to seek what you need. Don't try to push too hard, go with the flow and watch what happens

I like to put my seed thoughts, or mantras, on my phone. I mentioned earlier the app called voice recorder. I recorded my message and I will plug in my ear buds first thing in the morning, once during the day, and once again in bed before I go to sleep. Does it work? It sure does.

Doing these things in this book will help you in all areas of your life. If you put these ideas into practice, you will be able to see that the answers are always there if you just learn to tune in and listen.

4. Tuning in with visualization

Tuning in and doing what it takes to make the necessary changes, is one of the most important things you can do. You can have all of these tools, yet never use them. You have the power within. One tool that is greatly overlooked is the power of visualization. You must learn to use your thoughts and your mind, your conscious and your subconscious mind to see exactly what you want. You have to learn to spend time visualizing what you want. Get the visual picture so ingrained in your head that when you think about it for even a second you see yourself as having it already. It may seem like a tall order but it really isn't, just like anything else, you need to learn how to do this. And with time it will become second nature.

I like to sit with my ideas on paper and look at each one and say it out loud or quietly in my head and then start visualizing as having it right now. Whatever it is I desire for my life I see it and I daydream as having it, I feel it, I use all my senses to bring it to life. This plants the seeds of what I want to grow in my life. Then by watering it with visualization. It is nourishing it till it grows and becomes part of my life.

This exercise is again about quieting your surroundings and your mind getting in a place you can do this without being distracted. It's like setting your intentions but you need to spend time with your desire. You need to get that picture so deep in your thoughts, so real that you can see it crystal clear in your thoughts until you can pull that vision up in your thoughts in an instant. Take the time to do this often. Always kick out any negative thought that wants to try to take it away from you. You need to say, no way it's mine I believe and I receive it.

Don't let anything or anyone tell you it will never happen. There is a way, you might not see the way but there is a way, if you just keep it in your thoughts believe and never let it go. The more you put your positive wants into your thinking and really see this thought clear as having it now, the sooner it will become reality. Again, just make sure you don't miss the ways you are being shown to receive the thing you want. There are many different or unusual things you might have to do to receive what you need or want. Things that may not make any sense, just do what you feel lead to do. It may be what you have to do that will help you find what you want.

If you have a hard time seeing in your mind what you want, make yourself up a dream board or a little dream photo book. I have both. The little photo book I can take with me anywhere. I cut out pictures of what I want and then I placed them on a cork board or use a foam board. I put it in a place I can see every day. In my dream photobook I did the same thing. I cut out pictures and I placed a picture of myself in front of what I wanted. Or I took a picture of me doing something I wanted to do. I added a phrase to the picture, like I am a great speaker, or great writer, or vacations to Ireland and the places I want to visit. I wrote travel to all the places I want to see. Don't be afraid to put your dreams on your board. You need to take them out of the dark closet and into the light of day and put them in a place you can see them every day.

This will help you to be able to visualize your dreams. You will be able to see that picture from your board making it easy to see in your mind. Another good thing is watching a you tube video on what it is you want. Look into what you want just as if you will have it very soon. If it's in a store, go look at it, if it's a vacation go to a travel agent, if you want a house, then go look at houses. You have to make it reality in your mind. Do whatever you can to make it come alive in your thoughts. I call this dream building. Don't make an excuse. Excuses are your reasons why you can't achieve them. Do the work, forget the excuses.

Most people just think about what they want. They may talk about what they want but that is as far as it gets. If you just talk about it, that is all it will ever be. You have to start planning it and you will find the way will be made. You don't have to know the how at first, just keep walking in the direction of your dream and you will find the answers will appear and the way will be made. Just don't give up.

Once again, I have to keep going back to my quiet time with God/source. He is my source, I have to realize that I need my direction, my guidance, my strength, my courage from the source that makes all things happen. If I sit idle and do nothing, then that is what I will receive. When I get far away from my quiet time connecting to my source of energy, I become weak and discouraged. I will just go through life on auto pilot taking what is given to me and never receiving all the desires placed in my heart. They were placed there from someplace, know that you can receive them if you learn to do what is needed to receive them.

Connection is key. Without that I am constantly being thrown to and fro on waves I may not want to be on, thinking it's just the way it is. Stop listening to these negative whispers from the dark side. We all can have the desires of our heart when we learn to plug into our source and get charged daily. Just like a cell phone needs charging, we do as well. Being charged will help us keep going, doing what we are shown to do and help us receive what we desire. We can all have whatever we want if we just listen, do what we are shown and never give up. No matter where you are in life it is possible to change your life around and make it what you want. It's never too late.

I have given you some great exercises you can use to connect to the gifts within you. You can learn to use them, to help you in your day to day life. By doing simple things that help you daily, to tune in and hear what you need to hear, see and do. I know each is attainable. The thing that needs to be put in play for these things to take place is you, putting the effort into changing yourself to what you want to become. Don't you believe your worth it? There is no free lunch. It's simple but hard, and you are worth it. You have everything you need right inside of you. If you are willing to take the time and apply what you have. Apply what you are shown.

A couple of stories from my life using these exercises

I would like to share with you a couple of days in my life just so you can see how my life works for me. I want to do this because I think you need to see what I have to deal with daily. It's not a free ride. It takes work and determination to move forward. Most people have to work at things each day. Never look at someone and say they have it all together and they have everything they need to make things happen. That is not the truth. Everything takes work and is a daily process to keep things going in the direction you want to go.

I found myself in a place that I was trying to do my visualization seeing and saying I manifest what I wanted. I realized I couldn't see my goals. Everything seemed jumbled up. I felt unsure of my desires. I felt confused. These are the negative whispers that try to put doubt, fear, anxiety or worry into our thoughts. They try to stop us from the progress we are making. Sometimes you could say it feels like two steps forward three steps back. This day I felt all over the map and very unfocused like someone came in and switched the channel. I felt blown out of the water.

I opened a book I started rereading it and got a confirmation/synchronicity. I read "stick to your purpose (what you want) and maintain your faith and gratitude." I realized that second my mind got lost on what exactly I wanted, because of this stressful place I was in with money. I started to stray from my vision to a simpler way. That way had two different paths I could go. It got me confused because neither path was what I wanted. I went back to my little book of goals I carry with me (the little photo book I have pictures of me and all the desires I want along with the words, I have favor and I manifest what I desire.) I thought about exactly what I wanted and saw how I got off track because I allowed those negative whispers to come in and take control for a bit. I worked things out in my thoughts and got back on track with the desires of my heart. They hadn't changed, they just got lost for a day or two. Once I realized this, I took a few deep cleansing breaths and looked at my dream book and saw what it was I really wanted and got back on track with my desires. I said a word of thanks and forgiveness.

That is why I keep that little photo album with me. It helps me stay on track and focused. I was not looking at the little dream book for a few days, and was trying to do it without looking at what I wanted. For those of you who have a hard time staying focused, this is a great tool. I can still close my eyes and focus but it helps me see those pictures clearer than ever. Then, I can roll the camera from that point after seeing the picture.

There are messages in everything we see if we know how to look

One night I seemed to be waking up every hour, first it was 1:22 then 2:22, then 3:22, then 4:22. I seem to get numbers as well as books that try to get my attention. God sends these things to speak to me. The next morning after breakfast and a shower, feeling a bit tired with no reason to get up in the morning, I went into my office and looked at the eagle sitting on the tree next to its nest. It's behind my house. I put my glasses on and everything was blurry. I couldn't understand why so I took them off, and went into the room where my meditation pillows are and sat down, I looked at my phone before I got started and it was 9:22. I also sent my daughter a message, I'll share that message in a minute.

I then asked a question about receiving the money I needed. I was in a pickle and I needed to do something fast or go get a job. It was quiet on my pillows and I sat there for a while basking in the quiet. There are times I write as well as sit quiet, because I feel close to my source and guided at this time to my answers. I didn't feel like I had anything to write but I started to write anyhow. All of a sudden, I was given all of these ideas I had been working on over the years and things kept pouring onto my paper, as well as things I needed to be doing to make these things happen. There were fourteen things that I should be doing to make my desires come to reality that I wasn't doing.

I wrote "you have much to do so get going on them." "You do have a reason to get up in the morning. You have work to do. Why should you be given more work and ideas if you don't do the ones you have been given. If you don't get it together soon you will be out getting a job working for someone else. If you want to be good at being self-employed you have to do what you are being shown to work on, otherwise nothing will happen."

I was finished with my meditation, so I went to my computer and opened up an email that I was drawn to. It was about learning to be a freelance writer for places. I sent for their free guide. I asked and I got information. I got a lot of info from all the things I should be doing, to a place I could work and do freelance writing. If I felt the need to work for someone else. Yes! I did receive all the answers I needed to hear but did I want them? I was given choices.

I also got a message about the book I directed my husband to read, "The science of getting rich" by Wallace D. Wattles. He had listened to it that day. I was a bit taken by what he got out of the book. He got out of it that you should work with what you have and the things you need will be shown to you. I had also been rereading this book as well. So what did I get on my pillows in meditation that day? Fourteen things that I should be doing that I wasn't doing. Work with what you have. I wasn't working with what I had, I wanted more or something else. Why would I be given more if I wasn't using what I already had. Very simple yet hard.

So now back to the beginning of my story with the glasses. I'll tie all of these things together; God had shown me all of these things while I was spending quiet time with Him. He showed me the things I wasn't doing and should be doing, so I made a list. I then put my glasses on again, but everything was still blurry and I still couldn't see out of them. When I took a closer look at my glasses, I realized one lens had popped out and all of a sudden, I got the message.

Everything got blurry and you couldn't see all of the things I have been giving you. Things you aren't doing. You keep wanting more but you aren't using what you've already been given. Bam another message hit me, the science of getting rich, what Bob's take on it was "work with what you have right now" and the rest will be given to you.

When we aren't connected, we can miss all of these little insignificant messages. We don't know how to put them altogether. We are either not connected, disconnected, plugging in here and there, or we have never been connected at all.

Now here is the synchronicity about my daughter's text I said I would get back to, again we can miss these simple messages that are connected if we are disconnected. You won't see that this simple thing is giving you a message. I got this text before I started my meditation. I asked her about this friend that wanted to connect, she was supposed to give one of us a phone number, so I asked my daughter what happened. She said she gave me the number in that text message. All I saw was the lady's name. But because I am so great on the computer (not connected) I didn't realize I had to click on that name to get the information. I missed it completely. The phone number was right in front of me but because I didn't understand how to do it, I didn't get the info I needed. What you need to do may be right in front of you but because you are not connected you can miss the information you need to move forward.

I hope you can see what I am trying to say here. There are messages that come to you all the time in strange ways that we miss. When I am connected to God, I can see these messages come all the time when I am open to receiving them. I got all of this information in less than an hours' time. And as I was writing this all down one of the eagles was circling around my house. Eagles are a sign God uses to help reassure me that what I'm hearing is correct. He speaks to me in a number of ways. They are the ways I have always found that he uses just for me. I'm sure he will speak to you in ways that only you know he is speaking directly to you.

Head versus heart

I was thinking about this man who I admired and thought I would Google him. I wanted to learn more about him and where he stood on his beliefs. I read the article and it made me start thinking about some different things. I really don't want to go into detail about this man. I like him and he has a different take on what I believe. He has his path and I have mine. As in everything under the sun there is good and bad to every single thing. I'm not saying this man is bad, he just has different ideas than I have. It is what you do with it that makes a difference. There are a lot of good things in the new age believing, I have found a lot of good things, but I don't feel led to believe in some ideas.

In all things there can be good and bad. I choose what I feel is good for me and my path, and leave what I don't believe behind. I can say that about every area of my life. What I need on my path I will take and apply and what doesn't serve me, I leave. I have my journey and others have theirs. I take all I find and seek God for what I feel He is telling me and showing me, that is right for my path, and I move on. As should each one of us. We have to move in the path we feel is right for us and feels right with our connection to God.

Under the articles I read about him on Google, there was an article a religious woman had written that was condemning his belief. She was also condemning another great man, a Christian who is on his spiritual path and doing what God has called him to do and I like this man a lot as well. I really don't like that people are so ready to jump on someone else because it doesn't match up with what they believe. I try not to judge, it's not my job. This article brought me to asking questions. For me, I am a heart person. I go into my quiet space and I really seek God. I don't want to just quote things that I am taught from the Bible or from man, I need the answers from the Almighty God, period.

I have gone up against great scholars of the Bible, and was able to speak from the heart. This is my gift God has given me. I cannot remember all the scriptures in the Bible, I just depend on God to give me what I need when I need the answer. This has been what he has been calling me to do. Teach people to seek him with their whole heart. Not just with their head. You can have a lot of head knowledge without heart. And you can have a lot of heart knowledge without head. You need a balance. How can we do this? Seek him with your whole heart and believe that he will give you the answers you need. We are not to rely on what men teach. We are to go into our quiet place and there we will find just what we need.

Back to my thinking and pondering moment about this man. It wasn't just about this man; it was also about what people believe in, and how some people have such different beliefs. I was thinking about how to teach people to really hear the voice within that is God, and not mistake it from the beliefs they have been taught. Or even worse brainwashed into believing. How can people that have been taught to hate and kill for their religious beliefs be able to hear the voice of love. Or people that don't believe in a God be able to really discern good from bad. Even though I know God is calling me to do this, sometimes I have to know more so I ask and seek the answers I need.

I decided that I would just do what I always do and give all these things I was thinking about to God. This day I visualized putting them into God's hands and asking Him to deal with them. In the morning I woke up and was led to go to the Bible and get my answer. I thought, okay, this is going to take me to a number of places in the Bible. I opened it the way I do expecting God to give me the answer and as always, I was awed at what he showed me.

Mark 7: 6-9 (NIV)
6.These people honor me with their lips but their hearts are far from me.
7. They worship me in vain; their teachings are but rules taught by men.
8. You have let go of the commands of God and are holding on to the traditions of men.
9. You have a fine way of setting aside the commands of God in order to observe your own traditions.

And there was another scripture that jumped out at me when Peter was trying to rebuke Jesus for what he was saying. Jesus said in Mark 8:33 Get behind me Satan, you do not have in mind the things of God, but the things of men.

I thought these were so right on for what my questions were. I was looking at several people and their beliefs, and I was also looking at the evil thinking in the world to kill man for what they believe. It can be so confusing without seeking with your whole heart.

What did I get out of all of these things God was showing me? You must go within and search within to find your answers to your life. Ask and keep asking, seek and keep seeking, knock and keep knocking. God will answer you. If you do this, you will know his voice. For it is written in the Bible, "my sheep will know my voice." Sheep know their Shepherd's voice.

Learn to recognize the Shepherd's voice. This is the most

important thing we need to learn in this day, to know the Shepherd's voice. Listen to what the Shepherd is telling you to do and follow it. Remember the Shepherd wants to lead us and guide us in this world. He wants you to be on your perfect path. He wants you to be aware of wolves dressed in sheep's clothing that want to come and destroy you. In all the world right now, it is the most important. Hearing the voice within to guide you through this world. We need to get a handle on this because the battle is in our thoughts for good and evil. Choose who is controlling your thoughts and you're thinking right now.

Grieving and using your inner voice to help you through

I woke up this morning and could not get these thoughts off my mind. I felt I needed to share these thoughts with you. I have a bigger book that I have been working on for a while, but I felt the need to make a smaller book on just this topic, "hearing the voice within." I always receive confirmations or synchronicities when I ask questions. They came when I just so happened to pull out two books that are very powerful books that got my attention. They showed me to keep my book short. The significance of both of these books are they are both great books that are short and powerful. I always try to follow what He's shown me adding whatever He directs me to put into this book

I would like to share a little story about my daughter, Salina. She passed away when she was thirty-four. I have written and published a children's book about the time when she was four years old. She wanted to ride her bike without training wheels. She would do that the day she turned five years old, and she did just that. I named the book "Salina rides her bike – A true story of a little girl's determination to take off her training wheels."

When Salina passed away, she made sure she let me know she was okay. I'm not sure what it is all about on the other side of death but I will tell you she made sure I would be okay and that she was fine after she passed away. That was how she was. At that time, I didn't realize I could have been more in tune with her had I really understood I could go deeper into connecting to spirit within, and maybe I could have seen more from her. But I saw enough to know that she was telling me things from the other side.

After she passed away the first night we were at the funeral home she made herself known. I had put her little alarm drum set clock on the condolence cards table. That drum set clock didn't work, Salina had told me this when I packed it away when she moved. She said it didn't work but she still liked it because of who got it for her. When I put the clock down, I noticed the hands where going around, I thought that odd because it didn't work at all.

When we were all saying our goodbyes at the end of the night to go home that alarm clock went off playing the drum alarm. We all couldn't believe it and said hello to Salina and went home, feeling a bit like she was with us. When I came home that night, I set the drum set clock on our dining room table, the next morning, it went off again, before we went to the church for the service. Also, our thermostat for the heat was completely turned off. It was February, our thermostat never ever is turned off completely. Not even in the summer months. Again, I knew Salina was trying to tell us she was okay.

Several weeks later, I was talking with my son. I had wanted to go to Hawaii for my fiftieth birthday for a long time. Now more than ever I just wanted to get away. My birthday was in the beginning of June. This was still February. My son, said Mom if you want to go to Hawaii, then go. He walked out of the house and I turned to walk down the hall. Just at that moment, I saw a piece of paper fall to the floor, from the pile of papers I had to sort through from Salina's apartment. I walked over to that cabinet, bent down and picked up that paper and saw it was a postcard of Hawaii. I stood there in shock. Knowing that Salina was there speaking to me telling me to go to Hawaii. I am in awe of how things work. If we could just tune in to the unseen things of this world, and not be so afraid. I believe she was trying to tell me to go to Hawaii and it was okay to go. She also wanted to be a part of helping me to go. I believe she was saying "Mom, go to Hawaii!"

I didn't have the money to go to Hawaii at that time and I probably would have never gone. But because she came through and showed me in this way, I saw the way. I had some money left over from a small insurance policy I had to cover funeral expenses, I used that extra money and went to Hawaii.

I totally believe Salina gave me my trip to Hawaii for my fiftieth birthday. Through her persistence beyond the grave. And I believe that where she is, she is okay. I also feel that we should all go on in our journey celebrating the lives that have touched us. We can't control things we don't understand. These things should not paralyze us from living our lives, in grief and sadness. Our loved ones were here for us for a season and we should rejoice in the time we had to spend with them.

If you have lost a child or a loved one and you are having a hard time moving forward, find a way to get over your grief. Our thoughts are a powerful tool. You can take those thoughts and use them to hurt you or you can take those thoughts and use them for your good. You can live in that sadness, but what good does it do you to live in that place. It doesn't help you one bit. I truly believe that your loved one does not want you to stay in that grief and sadness. If you don't feel like living for yourself then try looking at it differently and live for them. Making them proud of you for doing the best you can. Be a better person because you had them in your life for a while. Make the best of your life. I am sure that they never ever wanted to cause you grief and sadness for leaving you. Let them soar, by being the best you can be and show them in a great way that you were happy to have had them in your life for the time you had them.

I look at it as I don't want to hold Salina back from where she is at, because I am sad and am grieving far too long over her passing. I want her to soar. I want her to be the best she can be. I don't want her to see me constantly grieving.

You were not born into this world to live a sad and unhappy life. Everything is in our thoughts and what we put in them. You cannot change the past so start looking at things differently and decide to be the best you can be. If you have to be the best you can be for your loved one, then do it. Start making the best life you can. Enjoy the other loved ones you have in your life. I tend to shower more love on the loved ones that are still here now in my life, because I am grateful, I still have love to shower on others.

If you don't have any relatives to shower love to there are many places that need your help that you can give your love to, in a good positive uplifting way. We all need love, we all want someone to care for us, and for us to care for others. There are so many ways that we can show our love and caring. Don't let that love, caring and kind heart die in grief and sadness. You have so much to give and I'm sure your loved ones would agree and are cheering you to do just that. Change your thoughts, change your thinking, change the way you look at life.

Look within and hear what that voice is telling you to do. You will be so glad you tuned in and finally decided to listen. Everything can be changed when we tune in, listen and do what that voice within is telling you to do. God bless the brokenhearted. Mend your heart today. Take the steps you need for the ones you've loved who have passed on, and the ones you love that are still here on earth.

More on the conscious and subconscious mind

Your conscious and subconscious mind is your total thought process, it is who we are, it is everything we think, do, say and how we act. I want to show you more on how to use this wonderful mind God has given us. It is how we can change all the things we don't like about ourselves.

Some studies say we use 5 percent of our conscious mind and the rest of our mind, the 95 percent, is our subconscious mind. Other studies show 10 percent conscious and 90 percent subconscious mind. Both studies are saying we don't use much of our conscious mind. They are about the same thing; one just makes your conscious brain work 5 percent less. The iceberg theory talks about 90 percent -10 percent brain use. But in my own unscientific thought does it really matter? When we learn to tune in and use what we have, that is all we need to overcome all things in life so we can have the best life ever.

It may solve a lot of explanations as to why we do the things we do. But I think that we need to realize just because they tell us we use 5 percent or 10 percent of our conscious mind and 90 percent or 95 percent is our subconscious mind. Don't believe that you cannot use both your subconscious and conscious to change your thinking.

I looked at a picture of an iceberg, it had the conscious mind as being 10 percent above water and the subconscious as 90 percent underneath the water. While I was in meditation God showed me something that I thought quite interesting. This picture was of our body, 10 percent above the water being our mind and thinking, it's like sticking our heads out and the rest of the body is hidden. Like a turtle sticking its head out and the rest of the body is hidden and safe, so we think.

The 10 percent is getting bombarded from what we hear, see and allow into that narrow passageway into our lives. What we allow in we will get back out. Yet all the power is hidden under the water and we fail to tap into it. We allow the 10 percent to rule us. There is only 10 percent the dark side can use to get to us and so we chose that side and what it feeds us. We constantly are feeding our mind negative, evil, even horrible things. We are so immune to these negative common ways of life, we don't see that they are making up who we are, and what we believe.

When we look at this massive iceberg, we should see the 90 percent, the subconscious, is taking in all the data that is right and wrong, and has so much power. When we learn the right way to tap in and learn how to use this power the correct way. We will learn that this power will lead, guide and direct us to the things that are good and the things we want for our lives. This power was put there from the one who created us. Our God, and He wants us to learn how to tap into all our resources built into our being.

Think about it the 10 percent sticking out of the iceberg is the brain, eyes, ears and mouth, the window to our soul. It controls all we do and all we say. What we see, hear and allow into our body comes back out, if it's negative it will come back out negative unless we start to make a change. We have to stop believing what the world is pouring into us. The scripture says, we will see and not really see, we will hear and not really hear. Mark 4:12 – They may be ever seeing but never perceiving and ever hearing but never understanding otherwise they might turn and be forgiven. We are allowing 10 percent that is above the surface to control this mighty vessel.

Over and over through the years I keep getting this scripture verse. Mark 4:12. And this is why God is telling me to "teach my people to seek me with their whole heart, mind body and spirit through quiet time with him." Take the time to pull your plug from the world and plug it into the source of life. To be filled with your source, your power, the right source of power. Not the worlds source of power.

There are so many sources of power in the world that fill us constantly throughout the day. It starts from childhood, plugging into the wrong source. We think it's cool, it's okay everyone's doing it, it's just the way it is. It's convenient to let our kids play these games, watch these shows. It really isn't what we should be plugging into. It is from the dark side filling our minds with garbage that's really worthless, taking up our time, controlling our thinking, making us miserable.

Tell me, do we learn how to take care of ourselves, for instance planting a garden to give us food? Do we learn how to help people, be kind and giving, do we learn respect? Could we survive in a time of crisis? I find that most of the games and TV shows are all about killing, being disrespectful, being mean, and hurting people. I really can't believe what I am hearing coming out of these games and I wonder how we as people can sustain this type of programming. What we put in we get back out. It's the way of the world but that doesn't mean it's the right way.

We need to learn the art of plugging into our source through quiet connection, and listening. We need to learn to hear and see what we need to know. Because if we don't, we will only know how to be controlled by man's ways and not the way we are to go. We will always be dependent on man to take care of us. Someone else to feed us. Someone else to plant the food, to reap the harvest, to kill the animals, to catch the fish, to make us dinner, to send our clothes to us. Hunting, fishing and farming are all becoming a thing of the past. No one wants to be bothered with it for many different reasons. It's a lot of work but it is a great craft to be able to feed yourself. They cry take our guns away, but the biggest reason to have guns and bow and arrows was to help us to feed ourselves. Not to kill people. What we should do first is take away these destructive games programming to kill. Get rid of the glory in killing other people and being the winner. Stop teaching how to solve a murder, on crime shows, which also shows you how to kill and get away with it. All of this negative programing we think is ok.

Is this programming catching up with us? I believe it is. How long can we keep going in this direction? How long will the media keep feeding us what they want us to believe before we start to see and take charge. Do you want to be the person in the scripture Mark 4:12 – They may be ever seeing but never perceiving and ever hearing but never understanding. We do have the answers lying within, if we learn to stop, be still and hear, listen and do. But we tend to leave out "do". When we hear the right things, know the right things, we must do the right thing and stop ignoring the "do the right thing" part.

I gave you two studies on one of the great powers within. Our conscious mind and our subconscious mind. A great tool that pretty much makes up our lives. We can use this power for the good or for the bad or not at all. It's your choice. By plugging in to your source the Great Creator, your God, you can do great things.

Let's go back and take a look again to what the voice within is all about. With all of this new age technology and other people's opinions bombarding our thoughts, we need more than ever to be connected to God. If we aren't grounded and connected, we will be tossed to and fro. We will never be grounded to what we need. We will never be able to make our own decisions. Because we will be listening to everyone else's ideas. It's so easy to hear one thing and believe it, then hear something different and believe that thing, and so on, changing our minds because we don't really know what we believe as truth.

People can convince us to do all kinds of things we might not want to do. This is why being grounded in our own thinking through spending quiet time listening and seeking the answers within, will help us. We will know and understand the right way to continue on our journey through life, without being influenced by what other people want us to believe.

It's not by watching television, news, social media, gaming, YouTube, or music with negative messages, that will help you through. It's high time we take a look at what is really controlling us. Add up how much time you spend doing these things and how much time you spend connecting to source in quiet time, your source of energy (God). This will determine where you're getting the right input. Where you are being led, guided and directed. A lot of us use the excuse I just can't quiet my mind and turn off all of this chatter. This is the battle we face in life that we have to overcome. Because if you don't, then you will always be ever seeing but never perceiving and ever hearing but never understanding. You will always be in the to and fro motion of life tossed by whatever life throws at you and never find peace or comfort. Sounds kind of like the way they describe hell. You will never win in life. Don't let this be you. Take control of your thinking.

Learning to connect and be secure to your own anchor in the storms of life is what we all must learn to do. It can be done. Just like with everything in life we must start by taking baby steps, start with five minutes a day, then go from there. If you need to start with a good guided meditation that leads you into quiet time, then start looking and listening to find the right one for you. There are many guided meditations out there to help you. Just make sure you don't give up till you find the right ones for you. Make sure that the ones you choose bring you into silence at the end in a reasonably amount of time. It is in the quiet that you will learn to plug in and recharge. Quiet meditation will help you run smoothly and in the right direction on your journey through life. There are also many places that you can go to meditate as well. If you want it bad enough, you will make it happen.

This is the care our body and mind need. Just like taking care of your car, you have to do maintenance on your car to keep it running smoothly. Plugging into your source (God) by spending quiet time so He can speak to you and fill you with all the right things. This will keep your body and mind running smoothly, and in control of every situation. Because your guidance system will then be in the perfect place it needs to be to lead guide and direct you in every moment of your life. You won't have to get to the end of your rope, beaten down so weary the only thing you can do is cry out to him for help, feeling lost and out of control. Don't be unplugged so long you have to be towed in or worse yet you blow your engine. Give yourself the maintenance you need daily. Find the guidance, the answers, you are seeking, they are everywhere and always have been. You will finally be in control of your life. When you do this, you will find every question you ever ask will be answered. You will know how to receive and understand and apply the answer. You will believe in something and it will come to pass, because you understand how your connection helps you apply the answers you receive. You will stand in awe of what you've been missing your whole life.

I will say this over and over again, God will speak to you in all kinds of ways if you just open yourself up to Him. Stop worrying what people say. You need to follow your heart. I have learned that and I am so much more at peace then I used to be. Connecting to the God source that lives in you is what you have been searching for your whole life. People seem to search their whole life for what will make them happy. They think that if they acquire material things that will make them happy. Or they will look everywhere for what they think will make them happy, content, and peaceful.

They will go to a pastor, priest, friend, coach, therapist asking them to please show me the answers. Show me the how. Show me what is wrong with me. Show me what is blocking me, what is the problem. We have to realize that we are missing our source of energy, we are not connected to the God source that lives within. We've taken God and His power out of our lives. When we plug in to the source we will get charged and we will have the energy to do what it takes for us to have a better life.

It's not in a pill, a church, a psychologist, a doctor. It lives within us, in the stillness of our mind. It is God and with his connection we will find that peace and feel contentment. We may think we have God in our lives because we go to church, we say our prayers we do good for others, or read and study the Bible. These are all good things we should be doing. But if you are still feeling bad then you need to take a strong look at your life. Are you really connected to God? Do you hear and feel things all around you in our Universe that are answering your questions or your cries? Do you feel that God is speaking to you all the time? Or do you feel like God is silent?

I just want you to know God is here and God hears us when we speak. He is trying to communicate to you. Sometimes it's in a simple way and sometimes it's in a huge way. He will speak to you if you let Him.

I can't say it enough, there are many ways God will speak to us. I'm going to talk again about your intuition and your subconscious mind and add knowing into the mix. First, I'll share a few stories so you can see how I hear and how I know. I was sitting on my meditation pillows in quiet for a bit and felt I needed to write what I was hearing in my mind. One of the things I wrote was that you don't finish what you start. When I was finished meditating and writing I went down stairs and I started talking to my husband. We were talking about work things and he was telling me how this one guy does not finish what he starts. It hit me-- there is my synchronicity. I don't finish what I start, so I need to start finishing things.

 The second thing we talked about was how several people were being very difficult to work for. They would come in and be very mean to their employees and dish out orders with no compassion for these people. After we were done talking, I went in and picked up a book and opened it to "Handling difficult People" -- Another synchronicity.

 I was sitting on my meditation pillows asking God to help me with my achy body and my friend called and asked if I wanted to walk to the waterfalls. I automatically said yes and thanked God. After that walk, my body felt great. These are just simple daily things that happen in my life every day. It can be a big answer or small answers but they are there. Yes! God is still giving us signs and wonders, if we are open to seeing them. With these signs comes a knowing. But if you choose to ignore these little signs you will not know what you missed out on. For me this time it was healing for my achy body.

Our subconscious mind, is such a big help to us and connects us to God. The spirit is living within us. The subconscious mind is part of that. Learning to use our subconscious as I've spoken about earlier will help us in so many ways. We can use it to find answers that lie within us. Clear your thoughts and start taking advantage of this great power, our subconscious mind. Your subconscious and intuition work together hand and hand.

Our subconscious mind works all the time. It never stops. It is even working when we sleep. When we are sleeping is a good time to put our subconscious to work. By programming positive thoughts and the desires, we want to achieve into our mind. Doing this work plants, the seeds to work on them all night long. This helps to change the things that we need changing to move forward, such as bad habits, wrong patterns, things that no longer serve us any longer, or wrong thinking. It can help us to lose weight, find something we've lost, find a solution to a problem, the list of things our subconscious can do for us, is endless. I believe it's one tool we don't use the way we should. Whatever the reason, I think that we could and should find ways to use our subconscious mind a lot more. We haven't been taught how to use our Subconscious mind. Its high time for us to learn how to use this great tool.

There are people that just have that natural ability to use more of their brainpower than others. It's not about who is smarter or who is not smart enough, it's about how we as humans can learn to do anything, we set our minds to. We are all born into this world with different likes, wants, and desires. We all have different talents and different things that make us happy. Some people are happier than others and some have a desire to accomplish much more than others. Some feel they like more material things than others and some people love living off the grid. We are all different, and come to this earth for different reasons. I don't believe for a second that we lack the brain power to help use accomplish what we truly want in life. If we can learn to tap into the source within to help us accomplish our desires.

I do believe that every living person comes to this earth for a reason and can learn to do anything with what they have been given. It doesn't have to be major things; it can be small things. But each one of us can learn something. I think that people need to be taught how to use this brain power connected to our God power. Using lots of persistence to go along with it, never giving up until you succeed. But we also need to learn to trust, believe and have faith. If we are really plugging in to our source, we will see things we never thought possible. We have to realize this, it says in scripture that Gods ways are not our ways, all things are possible to him that believes, we can do all things. We have to believe that it is possible when we are plugged in to our source. Believe in your source and also believe that because you are plugged in then you can do it. God needs us to believe in ourselves as well as in Him. We need both. We need that connection to move forward. He is waiting for us to fully connect to Him.

If you would like to get a little more knowledge about your subconscious mind you should read some of Joseph Murphy's books. He has written several books that I truly like, and has really helped me to understand our subconscious thinking. "The Power of Your Subconscious Mind" really helped me to see what our subconscious is all about. Other books, including "Think Yourself Rich", "The Amazing Laws of the Cosmic Mind Power", "Putting the Power of Your Subconscious Mind to Work", are all great books that help you use your subconscious to receive the things you need or want. I was drawn to his work. And was drawn to purchase each one of these books, the last was in a little tiny bookstore I would have never went into, but for some reason I was led there and went right to his book.

I was brought up on certain ways of believing. I have always been a strong spiritual person and I always will be. But with these books I felt like God was showing me that this deep spirit that lives within us can be used and understood so much more than you could have ever imagined. You can be a stronger person when you use these inner workings residing in you. You can be more connected to God. Have a stronger sense of knowing that there are many ways God works through us, and speaks to us. These inner workings will help you lead a better life by helping you find your answers, find your way through life and be more at peace. I feel I've become a much stronger spiritual person. By learning and applying more of these gifts. Using your subconscious to help you is a God connection. It helps you be more in control by having faith, belief and a knowing. When you put your belief in God, having this connection will help you feel so much closer to God.

I think so many people know God can, they just don't think that He will do it for them. They don't feel they are worthy of what they ask from God. I personally feel that that is one of the biggest reasons we fail to receive what we ask from God. I don't feel it has anything to do with not believing that God can do it, I think we pray and then walk away with doubt. We pray again and walk away doubting He will be gracious to us and grant us what we ask for. We doubt that our mighty God really wants to help us. We continually feel unworthy to receive from God what we ask for.

I also believe that there is so much negativity and so many naysayers out there that put doubt in our heads. Or even good people that feel they are giving you the right advice, but make you feel doubtful that God will do what you ask of Him. With all of the research I've done over the years, I feel we're missing all these connections we have to God that we do not use. We do not take the time to spend with Him listening. WE DON' T DO WHAT HE IS SHOWING US TO DO.

He shows us things and we doubt or we feel it's too hard or we say it's not going to work. We don't stand on faith and believe that God is strong and He works through us, to help us. To me that is very powerful. God is strong and can do all things and we can be strong and conquer if we will just listen and do what He is showing us to do. No matter how hard, how stupid or how simple it is. If we are seeking Him and listening to Him and feel we are connected to God, then we must do what He is showing us to do. Not a little bit, we must do all He is showing us to do. We could conquer every time. This is where we fall short.

There are many things that I felt I could not conquer in my life; I made all kinds of excuses why I could never accomplish the task. Sometimes I would start to do these tasks a little at a time and I would eventually look back and find that I did it. The very thing I thought I could not do, here I was doing the task with ease. I realized that, the other day. I needed to have a paper typed up fast, I grabbed my laptop and set to work typing the paper.

Several years ago, I used to tell my son, I just can't type that fast. I even bought Dragon speak to text because I had so many hand written book pages that needed to be typed. I found with Dragon, speaking to the computer would write crazy things I didn't say or what I was trying to say came out all wrong. Or I would not be able to think as fast as I could speak. I found myself typing to fix mistakes. The more typing I did the easier it became. Typing became easier than talk to text. So, I gave up on dragon and found myself typing and really enjoying it. I may not set the world on fire with my speed, but the speed I type is fine with me.

I learned comparing myself to others was not the right thing for me to do. I realized it stopped me from getting what I wanted accomplished. It even hindered me from getting started because I thought I could never be as good as others typing. Just remember you may not be like someone else, but you are good enough. Realize you will get better and better every day. It's your journey, accept who you are, don't compare yourself to others and work at your own pace to get what you want accomplished. Don't forget to give yourself a pat on the back for plugging along and getting the task done. You do have it in you to accomplish anything you set out to do. Once you realize this, start working on it a little at a time, plugging along till it becomes second nature. Before you know it you will have accomplished your task, your dream or desire or whatever it is you want.

You can have the life you dream of if you just take the time to stop and listen. He'll send just what you need. Stop, listen, hear and do what you know in your mind, body, spirit, and heart are telling you.

Running on auto pilot

Learn to stop running on auto pilot. We automatically allow the conscious mind to override the subconscious ideas to do the things we have already learned. We continue to allow the old habits or old patterns to control the way we do things. Therefore, we continue on auto pilot, which is our comfort zone, doing the same things all of the time. Putting thoughts into our subconscious mind daily will help change the thoughts we no longer want in our lives. The 5 to 10 percent seems small, but has a lot of power to override new thought patterns. With a little effort to change, we can do all things. Learn to use them together to change your world.

One way to help change and override our negative conscious thinking is to use the five second rule. Let's say you hear something like I have to go take a walk as soon as I wake up. Then you should do that right away. This is what the five second rule is. In the first five seconds, do what you feel you need to do. Don't let your conscious mind tell you that you don't feel like it. I don't like to get moving so fast in the morning. The only way to change your life is to reprogram your old habits and make new ones. Squash those old negative habits, before they can take hold and stop you from what you know you should do. When you hear your inner voice say go for a walk, go straight to your clothes and shoes, throw them on and ignore those negative thoughts trying to talk you out of going for that walk, run, or bike ride. You have to learn to tune into your thoughts in every aspect of your life to change it and take charge. It is work, you have to take yourself off auto pilot, but it can be done. Start taking notice of your voice within and learn to hear the positive things it is trying to tell you to do. Push out those negative thoughts in your conscious mind that are trying to keep you in the same negative place you know longer wish to be in. Work with that voice within, in your subconscious thinking and your conscious thinking. You have the power to take hold and take charge of your life. When you learn to tune in to the right voices telling you the right things, you will be so happy you're finally in control of your life

I have given you two studies on the great powers within. Our conscious mind and our subconscious mind are two great gifts that make up our lives. We can use this power for the good or for the bad or not at all. It's your choice. Plugged in to our Source the great Creator, our God, we can do great things.

Now let's talk more about the voice within. With all this new age technology and other people's opinions bombarding our thoughts, we need more than ever to be connected to God. If we aren't grounded and connected, we will be tossed all over the place. We will never be able to make our own decisions because we listen to everyone else's ideas and what they believe. It's so easy to hear one thing and believe it, then hear something totally different and believe that thing. We change our mind continually because we don't know what is true. This is the reason God wanted me to teach us to "Stop, Listen and Hear the Voice Within." To seek out the knowledge, we need to make the right choices and to know the difference between truth and lies.

How do you know that you know that you know? This is called knowing. You feel it, you sense it in that moment you just know that it is correct. But we allow the negative whispers to come in and take away our knowing. We then second guess, make excuses and let that knowledge of knowing what we should do slip out of our thinking. Let's face it, we all know what we should do – we can hear it a million times but we continue to make excuses. This stops us from doing the things we are shown to do. I am the first one to admit it. I know that I should exercise, eat the right foods, stay away from certain foods that harm my body and do the right things, but I don't always do them, or I do it halfheartedly. I know that I should do the right things in everything I do, like be kind, patient, caring, helpful, loving. I should not say negative things about myself and others but at times, I tend to let things rip when I am not happy. I know that I shouldn't but in that moment I don't care. That is wrong and I know it. Best thing to do is walk away from negative intentions, take a deep breath, and find peace.

I want to reiterate what knowing is. When you learn to stop, think, and listen you will know in your heart and your head what you should do. Again, you must take yourself off autopilot and start readjusting your old thinking to your new thinking, changing old patterns to new patterns that will control your life. When you are in a tough spot where your thoughts and feelings are all over the map, you must realize you can tap into your knowing. Simply by going within, finding that quiet place in your mind, and connecting to the resources within. Make it a priority to find a quiet place and meditate and you will find your true knowing. It's there, it has always been there you just have to learn to tune in and trust what you are seeing, hearing, and feeling. The more you do this the more in control and at peace you will be. You will find that it will get easier and easier for you to acknowledge what is correct and what is wrong. Tuning into yourself and all there is within is what you have always needed to do to get yourself on track with your life.

If you are always feeling uptight, unhappy, out of control, way too busy, stressed, or not making the right choices, then you have gotten away from your source. You need to connect and find that inner peace. It's there, but without making the time to be quiet and connect, you will only continue on this crazy path you hate being on. Wake up from this fog and get back on your path. Get quiet and go within. You will find your true knowing, find peace, and take back control of your life.

Wake-up call

One day I got a wakeup call. God was speaking to me loudly. How do I know this? I was following the promptings in my spirit. What I was feeling had to do with my health. Usually, when I get a flare up in my breast from drinking coffee, I quit the coffee and it goes away. This time was different, the pain didn't go away and I had this feeling I needed to go get it looked at, so I did. I ended up getting a biopsy and the results were benign. But still there was this prompting to remove it, so I did. My doctor told me they put these markers in your breast so whenever you get a mammogram, they will see that is the place you had something done. I was told they left one marker in there and when getting the cyst removed, they would take and put four more in there. I told her I didn't want those markers in there. She said, "OK, remind me when the time comes." Having been through something with my mom, I'll share quickly this story. The anesthesiologist put the IV in the wrong arm. I told him it was in the wrong arm and he said they would fix it before surgery. He forgot and my mom ended up coming out of surgery with a beet red arm, never being able to write with that hand again, unable to sign her own name. I decided the best way to remind my doctor was to put a note on my gown, which I did.

She really wanted to abide by my wishes, so she did not put the new markers in my breast, but she couldn't find the marker she left when she did the biopsy. She went back in a second time to try and get that marker out, while there she took more tissue from another area. She couldn't find the marker and felt maybe another time she could go back in and get it out. Long story short, she told me when they tried to get that marker out, they took more tissue out from that area. It was the high markings for possibly getting breast cancer. People get their breast removed to avoid all that fear, and not wanting to take a chance on getting cancer. She said, "had we not went back in to get that marker we would have never found that out." She told me she thought I was really connected because of how things turned out.

She knew through other talks we shared that I was in tune with myself. The reason I am in tune is because I'm learning that I have to tune in. But, as I've said, I tune in and I hear but sometimes I don't want to listen. I love coffee it doesn't love me. It hurts me and I drink it anyway. I'm not listening. Another thing I wasn't listening to was to change the way I eat. I've been feeling for quite a few years to change my eating to more fruits and vegetables. I bought a book, "Gerson's way." This clinic that puts people on this strict diet and lots of fruits, vegetables, and juicing. I even had a man named Sarto Schickel come to speak in my town. He wrote a book "Cancer Healing Odyssey" about his wife and her using this diet to heal her from stage 4 ovarian cancer. I would try to eat this way for a while, and then I would stop.

For a while I was being shown that I needed to follow a healthy eating plan. God was trying to get my attention to listen. I was in the middle of the 8-week Skinny Genes Program by Debra Hollinrake at the Tree of Life Health Wellness Center on tapping/the Emotional Freedom Technique. In doing that course, I felt strongly to change and eat more fruits, vegetables, juicing and eating in line with Gerson's way. Everything was pointing to changing the way I eat.

Not to mention that through the years the weight kept coming on more and more. Praying, seeking, mediation, writing, all my promptings, urges, and feelings were saying change the way you eat. Unfortunately, we as people can be very stubborn and ignore all the signs sent to us. God didn't give up on me. He kept sending me signs. Now I get it. Listen to me or you will not be happy you didn't. The signs are very clear, and I shouldn't ignore them another second.

But when we go through sickness or have an ailment, at that time we hear it, the voice within, we decide that we are going to change. We feel in that moment we have been shown it can get worse if I don't take heed to the signs I am being show. But those negative whispers always seem to creep back in and make us weak and bring us back to bad habits or feel negative patterns. I wanted this to be the time that I finally took charge of my body. I could see that continuing down this path was wrong for me. I need to do what I am shown to do or suffer the consequences. Simple yet hard.

Every time I have gone through these unpleasant situations, I have found there was a lot of lessons I learned from each experience. Each time I can see there have been a number of signs that are all around me trying to show me what I need for my life. I need to start choosing the right ways to live a healthy, happy, successful life. I must stop procrastinating, stop waiting, stop making excuses, listen and obey my inner voice once and for all.

Sickness and harboring ill will

I am going to share another story about sickness in my life. I hope that sharing these stories will help you to understand how hearing the voice within can help you in every area of your life. God sure does give me a lot of stories. Probably because I tend to "not listen."

This story starts with vertigo. I have had vertigo attacks for a number of years and being, who I am, I wanted to find out the cause. This particular day was day seven of vertigo, and I was having enough of lying on the couch feeling dizzy. I wanted to get rid of it. I was getting a little better but not one hundred percent. As I always do, I started asking questions as to why I have this vertigo and why its hanging on so long. (Notice I say this vertigo instead of my vertigo, I will never claim a sickness as my own, it's not mine, I don't want it so I'm not claiming it as mine. And I believe it will go away forever.) I thought that I had found the reason I get vertigo and I thought it might come from changes in the barometric pressure. It kind of made sense to me – something with the pressure change and the crystals in your ears get out of whack. But as I always do, I am always asking for the right answer.

I sat down at my desk and felt led to open this little booklet I have "The Power of Positive Thinking" by Norman Vincent Peale. I opened the booklet up to Chapter 10 "When vitality sags try this formula". I started to read it and the revelations started pouring over me. The words could not be clearer to me, if you don't feel good, ask yourself if you are harboring any ill will, resentment, or grudges towards someone. He was saying that this bad feeling isn't hurting the other person, but these bad feelings eat away at you, making you sick, sapping your energy and deteriorating your health and your happiness. Emotional ills turn in upon yourself, harming your body.

Anger, resentment and guilt make you sick. I'm sure it does a lot more to you as well. He also talked about the Holy Bible still being the most up to date book on your wellbeing, and the booklet went on to give you suggestions to get rid of these bad feelings and replace them with good feelings.

This little booklet was so right on, it said to look at what was bothering you if you weren't up to par. So, I went back to the day I started feeling the vertigo taking hold of me. It was a Saturday, Labor Day weekend. I was feeling a bit unhappy that we didn't go to the shore for the two days prior to the holiday.

We were tight on money. I accepted it, but come Friday, I was feeling we should have saved money to go even for just one day. The trip was cancelled. I felt a little sad about not going and tried to accept it. Each of those 4 days, we stopped someplace in our town and spent money we could have used for a day at the beach. I think that unconsciously, I was harboring ill feelings that we didn't take the money and go on a day trip to the beach but spent money at places I didn't want to be at.

Trying to be the best I could be with the situation. I thought I was dealing with it in my mind but the unconscious mind was not having it. It started rebelling and I started feeling the consequences of keeping everything bottled up. I felt annoyed that we could spent money at these places, but not go to the beach. It wasn't just once, it was four times, and I guess I must have been harboring resentment and it showed in my health. Saturday, I started feeling the vertigo and it kept getting worse till I was on the couch not being able to lift my head up without being sick. I had the vertigo going on twelve days straight, and I ended up with a really bad UTI. It was so painful, it made me sick and I believe it was causing the vertigo flare up. I was down for the count for over a month. Louise Hay has some great books I love "How to Heal Your Life," so I decided to look at what her meaning in her book said about my health issues. It said UTI was from being pissed off. Vertigo was not moving forward. I had both of these. Louise's references were right on. I do have a problem moving forward and I was quietly pissed off we didn't go to the shore. I bottled up all these emotions and kept them inside of me. Thinking I could just push them deep inside of me and eventually forget about them. To all of you out, there just know that you can't fool your body by not dealing with things in your life. They will eventually show their ugly head in the form of sickness.

I think that they work in combinations with the things you do that you know you shouldn't do. I will explain in my case how this works. I like coffee a lot and I have said that before. I really love coffee. It doesn't love me. I have been drinking coffee since I was three years old, and I have had to stop drinking coffee. But I will try to beat the odds and believe that this time I will overcome it and finally be able to drink coffee. But guess what – it will catch up with me every time. I will tell you I have tried this for most of my life. I guess maybe this time I really need to take heed and give it up.

Why do I believe that this works in combination? Because I have found that I can get away with drinking coffee for just so long. Then, I will have a situation come up like this one where I bottle up all of my negative feelings and emotions and not deal with them. Suddenly, everything comes crashing down and it comes in the form of sickness. Drinking the coffee is hurting my body, adding stress from not dealing with negative feelings leads to sickness. Sickness is something that we don't even realize can be caused by a lot of stress along with eating the things we love such as coffee, sugar, processed foods, alcohol, cigarettes, drugs, and so many other bad things. When we put bad things into our bodies, bad things come back out. If I would only try to do my best to deal with stress and stop adding bad stuff into my body, I would live a lot healthier life. We all need to realize this and do what is right to have a healthy happy life.

You might think I am crazy and wonder how I know this. When I drink coffee, my lower back hurts, yet I put up with it because I love coffee. That little taste means more to me than not having that pain in my back. Sometimes I can go on like this for a long time. But when I started bottling up emotional things that bothered me, and didn't deal with them, my body starts to rebel and sickness shows its ugly head.

You can say to me, why do this to yourself? Why put yourself through this? Because I love coffee. It is a part of me that I am having a hard time giving it up completely. I feel like it's coffee, everyone does it, why do I have to stay away from it? It's not fair. Why me? It is what it is, and I must once and for all listen to my body. This has not been the first time. I pray it is the last time. and I finally deal with these things negative things that harm me, I need to stop trying to override what I know as truth. Certain drinks or foods I must avoid, plain and simple. Sugar is another enemy of the body we should all eat a lot less of. But we choose to stay blind to the effects sugar causes in our bodies – cancer being one of the main sicknesses caused by too much sugar, not to mention that too much sugar causes obesity.

Do you think this time I should listen to what my body is saying? Thank God He never gives up on us. Because we don't listen to His promptings, we can get off track. Getting off track may end up leading us through things we don't want to have to go through. Like these sicknesses that seem impossible and make us cry out, "why me, God?" Most of the time, if we would listen to these promptings, we wouldn't have to go through these awful times.

If you would really think about the sicknesses you are dealing with, you would find that you probably had emotional baggage you were avoiding as well as things you were putting into your body. Your body speaks to you all the time, but we humans will ignore the signs. We don't want to do the things shown to us that are right for our bodies. This is redundant, but I need you to get the point. My voice within is constantly telling me over and over don't eat or drink coffee, sugar, processed food, and other things that harm my body. I like them, so at times I ignore the warning signs that God is showing me. Don't let that be you any longer, take heed to what your voice within is telling you. You know that voice, and you know what it's telling you to do. Stop avoiding that voice. Start listening and do what it is telling you. You will be so glad you did. God, the Universe, angels and all the things He uses to help us hear Him and guide us through this journey called life. The right path we are to travel is here for all of us to reap if we just learn listen and do what He is calling us to do. I always say, "simple yet hard."

Once I saw this, I went back and started looking at the other times I got sick or had health issues. I found that I was harboring feelings that I was not dealing with as well as making poor eating choices. I thought I had logical answers as to why I had the health issues but that was only part of the reason. They were logical explanations that seemed to make sense. But God showed me the real reasons we get sick and it has everything to do with harboring emotions of anger, resentment, guilt and what we put into our bodies, just to name a few.

Once we see this and start seeking for the correct answers to all of the questions we have, will we be able to see exactly what is bothering us creating havoc in our mind, body and spirit. Realizing this produces sickness in our body. I also started looking at my loved ones and I could see why they got sick as well. I could only see from the outside why they got sick but if I had known this back then I may have been able to help them heal from the inside. Helping them to live a great life.

If you are wondering how you can get to the bottom of sickness, or what is ailing you, start by grabbing a pen and paper. Go back to the time you first started having the problem and write down everything you can think of, and you will find your answer. They may have been building for years making you sicker and sicker. Just remember, you can't fool your inner self. You may think you can but you really can't. After you do this, it is time to let them all go – never taking them back into your body. Learn to ask if that feeling or harboring thought worth it? You will realize it is not worth one minute of your time, replace it with good thoughts, send up a prayer for that person you hold ill will towards, and get back to living a good, happy, healthy, fulfilled life.

Take charge of your life and make your life the best life ever. Let go of the past, live life the way you feel you want your life to be, don't harbor ill will, speak up as to how you feel, and let go of things that don't serve you anymore. Most of the things we harbor are not worth it anyway. Just let go and give them to the one who can take care of them. Don't give them and take them back. Really release them. You will feel so much better and so much weight will come off your shoulders. You will feel so much healthier and happy.

More about my eagles

As I said earlier, a pair of eagles came and made their nest behind my house. They were giving me messages and promptings in my thoughts from seeing these eagles used by God. They were showing me things I needed to know. I used to see the eagles all the time being a bus driver, when I was in deep thought about something contemplating the answer, I would receive a sign. In that very moment, I would see an eagle or a pair of eagles. My heart would soar and I would smile and say thank you God. One time I was helping someone with their life goals, as I was driving up the road we looked up. Right in front of the bus was an eagle, claws down, hovering above us in the road just above the bus. We went right under that eagle and it didn't move. It was a "wow" moment, one I won't forget and that made a huge impression on me and my friend as well. The voice speaks in ways we don't understand. If we are not in tune with it and the universe, we will miss those split-second signs or confirmations.

I am also drawn to red cardinals for answers. They have always been around to help me with answers. I can be deep in thought for an answer and one will come right in front of me just at that moment I needed a sign or confirmation. There were times when I have had birds upon birds fly in my path while driving - in front of me and all around me, it would last for miles and miles and days and days. I would know the answer and that I wasn't alone. I have angels all around me helping me guiding me. You are no different than I am, once you start to fine tune, listen, and hear. You will learn that these things are here for all of us and we are not alone on our journey. You will better see and understand the signs that are all around you speaking to you.

You may have things like red cardinals, or eagles, or butterflies, dragonflies or something that also comes around just when you need it. It can even be a woodpecker hammering on the side of your house, I've had this happen as well. I'd like to stop and take a moment for you to think about this and write down what you feel that may be there to help you.

EXERCISE: WRITE DOWN SOMETHING OR THINGS THAT HAVE SPOKEN TO YOU.

You will find in doing this exercise how many times God has sent you signs but you have failed to see them. Keep your little notepad around to jot these things down daily as well.

God sent His Angels; they are all around us guiding us

How many times have we heard this? There are angels all around us, but do we honestly believe it? If we knew that angels were walking with us, then why don't we try to communicate with them. I think because we don't believe it 100 percent, or because we are afraid. These little feelings or whispers may be the angels communicating with us.

When my daughter passed away and she was communicating with me, I didn't try to communicate with her because I didn't understand. I saw the signs, I knew it was her and I did something with what she showed me, I went to Hawaii. At the time I didn't really know how to communicate with her. We are taught communing with the dead is wrong. Yet I knew in my heart that these signs were from her. I knew in my heart these were good signs from her. It was love from my daughter, because she cared so much in her own way and she wanted me to know she was okay and she wanted to do something nice for me after she passed away. When we tune in to God, the universe, and all this power within He has put here for us to use, the signs will become clearer and it won't be so hard to pick up on what we are being shown. It will become a healthy better way of life finding our direction and not feeling so alone, lost, and out of control.

I read the other day about a little boy who passed away and he was told by God he had to go back and share what he saw, "that there are birdies (he was only three and that was his word for angels) all around us, helping us. They talk to us as well. But we don't hear them the way we should." I've read about many near death experience stories, and they all say the same thing. Near death experiences are when people have died and came back to share what they had experienced. They say there are angels all around us helping us and guiding us. Yet we don't even try to take the time to quiet our thoughts and tune in to what God has put here on earth to connect us to Him and His guiding love.

We can lay out a shopping list of things we ask for without even once taking the time to listen. We allow the dark side to take that away. The connection to our source, our connection to what we need to lead healthier, happier, prosperous lives.

People walk around totally defeated. They don't care, because life has just become too hard. There was a movie I watched where the Israelites were slaves. Day in and day out they would get up and do hard work and didn't have a good life. As I was walking in the store the other day, I took a good look at people and how they were going about their business working. It didn't seem like they looked any different than those slaves. No, today we are far from what the slaves went through, but in the faces of these people they had the same blank look. They looked like they were so unhappy and couldn't care less how they were doing their job. They were there to do their job and that was it, as they were just going through the motions.

We need to be awakened again that God is powerful and He has sent His Angels. They are all around us to guide us. He has given us so much power that we could tap into if we open up and see. There are voices all around us trying to communicate, but instead we have the lights out sign on, no one is available. We have given up and we don't even realize it.

Most people don't go to church anymore. What's the use? They feel they only get judged, condemned, and they want your hard-earned money. The message is all about, "you are judged and condemned, and you will go to hell if you don't follow the commandments." You're condemned and judged already because no one can live up to what they are preaching. Yet the preachers are falling down in the same sin they are preaching about. People don't see anyone being the light and love of God. They don't feel like God is love, so how can we be love. They don't feel God in church, so why should we just go there and go through the motions. They feel like there is no use in wasting their time. I can have God at home. I don't get condemned or judged or told what I need to do. It is just fine staying home. The world is getting further and further away from God and the dark side is so happy keeping unity out of our lives. It is working overtime, just as it is written. We walk around defeated and ready to fall at any second. The things we are connected to are dark and evil. We are so far away from good and accept evil as just the way it is. Everyone is doing it, so it must be okay.

What is the great awakening? It is to find God in our hearts again. To wake up our hearts, our ears, our minds, and our eyes to see that God is everywhere. We just need to take the blinders off and the earplugs out of our ears. One by one, we put the blinders on and in turn we are getting away from our source, our energy, our charge and life itself. All it takes is a simple devotion by taking some time to be quiet. Spend some time communing with our God the source of all things created. No matter what you believe. No matter your journey. It's time to wake up, get your recharge, and see how wonderful life is when you are connected.

You are not alone. He has not left you alone. The only reason you feel like you're alone is you've lost your quiet connection time. You need to charge your life's battery every day. If you feel that you just can't do it, you can't sit because you are to antsy then you are defeated. You are letting the darkness take over. I heard Joel Osteen say something the other day that really struck a note. He was talking about entering rest following labor. Labor is not easy, it is hard. But it is necessary for us. You have to labor at work for a paycheck, you have to go into hard labor to give birth, you have to labor to make anything happen. You must realize that it says in the Bible you must labor into His rest, and that is through quiet time. It will be hard but it will be so worth it. I'll say this over and over, when I don't take that time to enter into His rest, I am so out it. I'm off balance, or I don't have it all together. I don't perform at my peak because I have not recharged my mind, body, and spirit to be my very best. It opens the door for the negative dark side to come into my thoughts like a thief, stealing my life, my confidence and my happiness

There are so many ways with the computer and internet that you can get help in anything you set your mind to do. There are lots of meditation videos out there that will lead you into quietness. You can search until you find the perfect one that works for you. When I am having a hard time, I will put on my earbuds and close out the world and listen to one of these guided meditations. I make sure I choose one that brings me into that quietness.

I also do worship that brings me to quietness. I do yoga that brings me to quietness. I also find that if I wake up a little earlier in the morning, sit up in bed, or go sit on my meditation pillows, I can enter into a time of connecting – I'm still in that sleepy, drowsy state and I can make it into my quiet time pretty quickly. I will say a few things in my mind asking God to speak to me. If I have a question I ask, and what I love when I'm done is to grab a pad and pen and start writing, I'll write the question and the answer will flow. If I don't have a question, I will just start writing and things I need to know will pour out onto my paper. This is quiet time; this is the rest we need to enter. Without it, we are lost sheep looking for our shepherd. The wolf will come and draw us away from our shepherd with all kinds of reasoning to keep us far away from the shepherd that watches over us and protects us from all bad things.

I have tried to cheat by staying in bed, but that only keeps me sleeping and I don't enter that quiet state that I need to be in. It is the art of stating that I am making the effort to enter quiet time with God. You will find the difference when you do this. There is sleep time that can be used for answers and there is quiet time to recharge you and help you find answers. You will know the difference and God knows the difference. You just can't cheat. For a season, I was getting up at 4:45 because I had to be to work within that hour. I still chose to get up fifteen minutes earlier and spend that time in quiet meditation.

If you can, stop right now and take this time to enter quiet time. If you know how to still your mind and keep it there, then do this now. Make sure you have a pen and pad to write after you are done. If you need some help, find a meditation that will help guide you to total quiet. There are several great apps out there for guided meditation. I use Insight Timer app. It has many great guided meditations and music for all your needs and when you are done start to write. Remember this is the labor to enter rest we so desperately need.

You will find each day you do this it will get better and better. You will find so much more and be more fulfilled. Remember though, just like exercise, it can be a challenge to do it daily. Make it a part of your life and you will find your world will change for the better. You will find you will feel happier, healthier and more in control of your life.

Opportunities we miss because we fail to see the signs set to us

I had been praying to God for years for the same thing. I would pray send me someone to help me. What I finally realized was God was sending me people. Most of the time I just wasn't seeing it. I would write in my journal, "wow, God showed me this idea or He sent me a person to help me." I'd write down, "He sent just what I needed." I came to the realization I would see He did send me things, I would acknowledge it, but I wouldn't apply it. I would let these things slip by me. I would feel like this was not the answer that I needed. Or I would find some lame excuse for not doing what he was showing me.

One day I finally looked at this. I had all these things being sent my way and I would let any excuse get in the way. People were saying to me here's my card call me I will help you. There has always been one thing that I feared and that is calling on the phone. Back in the old days, we would call it the hundred-pound phone. I would make up all kinds of excuses. Now is not a good time, they'll be busy... I would let these excuses stop me. Finally, I said I'm going to pick up the phone and call. After I started to do this, I realized that it wasn't that hard at all. To my advantage, these people truly wanted to help me. I was letting all this imagined fear stop me from getting the help I needed. Worse yet, I was asking God, He was answering, and I was not using the help He was sending me.

Are you asking and people keep coming into your life to help you? Or, are you seeing things placed in front of you to attend, like a club, seminar, workshop, or meditation class? This is your answer or sign. God is sending you the help you are asking for. For those of you who don't believe in God, your feelings hunches are all from God. Even though you don't believe in Him, He still believes in you. He will always put stuff out there to help you or keep you safe from harm, all you need to do is tune in.

I had a dream about everything being interconnected. A few days later, all of these thoughts and ideas I was having started making sense to me. The light bulb went on. I realized that God was showing and directing me to what I needed and to follow up on all my leads. I needed to trust Him, trust my instincts, and do what He was showing me. I think that it may even be a test to see if you have faith and are willing to do what He is showing you. You may go talk to a person or go to a workshop, club or whatever it is you are being shown, and it will lead you to what you need. Sometimes, it may even take a few times following a lead that will be just what you need. Follow all the leads you are given. One of them will be just what you need. It is that simple and yet that hard. Try and look at it like this, if you do nothing you will get nothing. What do you have to lose? A quote from Albert Einstein: "If you always do what you've always done, you'll always get what you've always got."

Don't let this be you. If this is you, then now is the time to get on with it and go after every lead that is shown to you. If you do this and never give up, you will find all the answers you need to succeed. All the things you need will be shown to you so you will accomplish your dreams. I think this can be applied to great health as well. Feeling lead to eat right, take supplements, exercise, or whatever strong urge you feel could be just what you need. Again, it can be that simple yet that hard. Doing what we know we should do seems hard, but remember, it is only in your mind. Start with baby steps and never give up.

We have to tune in and apply. If we don't, we will continue

down this road of discouragement and defeat our whole life, missing what we crave. We'll keep thinking that what we crave is out there somewhere, and not knowing how to get what we so desire. Once you learn this you can move forward and feel so much happier and content. The saying "it's not about the destination, it's about the journey there" is true. The journey can be about struggle, strain, and full of discontentment. It can also be about moving forward with ease using the leads you are sent. This will get you to your destination in a better frame of mind and you will enjoy it more once you do this. You will also know that the next journey you take will be even better.

Think of it like a treasure hunt. When you are out looking for treasure, you must look for the clues and keep going until you find your treasure. Each thing that is shown to you is a clue. You can either follow it to find the next clue or you can ignore it and therefore never find your treasure. You've got to decide which it will be. Will you ignore the leads or clues and just give up never finding your treasure, or will you use every clue you are shown until you finally find your treasure?

We all have the tools; it's how we use our tools that count. Some of us have more tools than others, I'm grateful I have all my body parts in working order and that my brain works well - these are gifts I am blessed to have. There are others who do not have these blessings that go a lot further than I do. Because they have that, "I can do spirit" that doesn't let anything get in their way. We may look at these people we see on these reality shows and be in awe of them. Tears may come to your eyes; you may cry your eyes out at their sad stories and of their disabilities. They have come through great challenges. So, what's your great challenge or disability? What is holding you back from making your dreams come true? Is your challenge a true disabling handicap like these awesome people, or is it just an excuse or fear you can't seem to overcome?

My challenge has always been fear and a lack of persistence that causes me to give up to soon. When I see these people with great challenges, I look at mine as a drop in the bucket. I'm not saying my problems are less real – by no means. I use these great people as heroes, and I say they did it and so can I. They have greater challenges and kept going and so can I. If they have what it takes, so do I. When I see them up there winning at their goals, I cry because they didn't let their challenges get in the way of having what they wanted. They worked hard to get there. They may have had many more struggles than I have, but they didn't let it stop them.

Do you put famous athletes or famous singers on your wall to inspire you? Are they helping you make your dreams happen? If not, try putting pictures of challenged people on your wall. Let that person be your hero. Let them inspire you. You may be looking at these famous people who have accomplished much, not having the same kinds of struggles. I'm sure that each one had many challenges to overcome before they got to where they are. You put them on your wall to look at, to inspire you. But you may develop excuses and tell yourself that they are so much better than you, they are so good looking, slimmer, smarter, they have more talent, better connections, they have... Add your excuse. You let all these excuses build up in your mind about the heroes you put on your wall to inspire you and in turn, you let these excuses stop you.

Instead of putting a famous person without physical challenges on your wall, find another hero. Put up a picture of someone who is physically challenged that has accomplished what you want to do. Let them be your inspiration. Let them help you to overcome anything that gets in your way. You can look at them and see a great hero, for they have overcome lots of things that you have never had to. You can look at them (without tears in your eyes) and see that they are brave, strong, persistent people. They had a dream just like you and didn't let anything stop them from getting what they wanted. We have the tools to help us to overcome. Don't let excuses get in your way. I have worked with special needs kids. They have so much to offer and are such an inspiration. They learn to do all kinds of great things. Be grateful for all you have and don't let excuses stop you from doing what you want to do.

Explosive blessings

I'm going from clues to find your treasures, to putting the right heroes on your wall to inspire you, to explosive blessings. This may encourage you to keep your eyes out for the signs all around you. People say God doesn't send signs anymore. I beg to differ with that statement. I see signs all the time, as I have shown you in this book. Answers and the way they come to you are signs.

I would like to share a story with you that, in my opinion, was a huge sign from God. When you learn to put these things together, you will see they are not just coincidences. I was listening to a series of messages by Joel Osteen. I really like Joel. He helps people to stay up and positive. It is his mission in life to do this – his calling, his journey. There are way too many miserable, unhappy, and defeated people out there that need that positive message.

At the time, I was in one of those hard places. As I was listening to his message, driving in my car, it was helping to lift my spirits. I was really feeling that the message was right on for me. I was so excited I felt like God gave me this message I thanked Him for it. All of a sudden, Joel said, "God will send you explosive blessings." Before my very eyes, a shooting star shot across the sky, right in front of me, and exploded. I knew that God sent that amazing exploding star and those special words straight to me in that moment. I remember the exact place and time. I felt like God had just came down and touched me with this amazing natural firework display and Joel was being used to give me the message God wanted me to hear.

When you learn that God has never left you and He does send His signs to you. All you have to do is take the time to put them together and receive these signs as answers. You'll find you are never alone. He has not left you or forsaken you, you have just gotten away from communing with Him, spending that much needed quiet time with Him for His direction and guidance. If you have never learned how to do this, then I suggest you learn. Draw near to your power, your source, your energy, and the Universe and all the vastness around you that God uses to help you. It's that simple voice within that will open a new and better world to you. The thing you've always searched for is within you, take the time and find it. That connection that will help you in every area of your life. Make the time and find that connection and let Him guide your life right now.

I'm so glad I have let Him into my life in this way. I will never be the same again. I am growing in leaps and bounds. I'm far from perfect and the road is not always easy, but I am so glad I'm never alone. I have someone to always commune with and who always has my back. He shows me all the time what I should be doing, giving me signs, and He never gives up on me, even when He knows I'm not getting it, or I ignore, block, or have pity parties, He will always send me what I need until I finally decide to see it and receive it and do it.

Stop worrying what other people are saying or doing. Stop condemning people for being on the path they are on. Stop all the negative hatred as to who is right or wrong. Start looking within to be the best version of yourself staying connected to your source and all God has put here for you to connect to Him. You will find you will become His light of love. You will no longer allow negative garbage to steal the life you were meant to live. Be a light unto the world. The light of love.

Seeing the other side of situations

This topic is coming up over and over to me therefore I know it is something I need to share in this book. I will only hit on this topic briefly, because this could be a whole book all by itself. I try to follow what I am being shown, and to obey what I am called to do. I'm going to talk about relationships. Not just to your significant other but to everyone – friends, family, acquaintances, coworkers, and strangers as well.

I can't tell you how many times I have heard or saw this happen. There are so many people who feel they are right in their point of view, that they will not in any way see the other person's side of the story. They will not admit that they could be wrong or part of the problem. When two people are not connecting to each other over a situation, it can never be resolved with one person being 100 percent right. You can't excuse your reasoning away if you are unwilling to try and see what the other person is seeing in your actions or what it is you are saying.

I have had this happen to me many times. In some cases, I can see something or get something totally different out of a situation. I can see what I see and not really see what the other person is seeing. That's why I like to ask lots of questions so I can get a better perspective on things. I have seen over the years many people part ways because they can't or won't try to see what the other person is seeing and feeling. It is simple yet so very hard. If you want things to work out, you must look at the problem or situation through the eyes of the other person. That is where you really need to spend some quiet time and ask for your inner voice, inner feelings inner guidance, the God source within to help you deal with this out of control situation. If you don't, it will end up in disaster. It is very sad to see people part ways when many times the things that make them part ways are simply not being able to see what the other person is seeing, feeling, and hearing.

If you could just learn to introspect and start seeking God to show you the other side through quiet time, you will find out it can be resolved and worked through. With kindness, patience and some work. If we would stop letting the negative whispers come in, take root, and destroy our relationships. This may come as a surprise – but we are not always right! We don't see things the way we need to see things all the time. We both may be right and both wrong because each person will see it in a different light.

Once we hear what the other person is saying, we will probably be shocked. They are telling us something that is totally different than how we are seeing the same situation. Do your best to understand how they are seeing it in their way. Work through your different viewpoints. Everyone has a different take on what they see and hear. Explaining both sides of what each is hearing, seeing, and feeling will amaze you both.

Learn to seek, hear, listen, and do. It is the best thing that can be done to resolve your differences. Next time you have a disagreement, take a moment to ask, "this is what I am hearing, seeing, and feeling. What do you see, feel and hear?" You will find that what you think you know or hear isn't what the other person is sending out. Communication is key to great relationships, and if you aren't willing to do that, then your relationships will never be the best they can be. That means all relationships, kids being one of them. Kids can hear and feel things that are totally wrong. If you fail to stop and talk over the situation, things can and do build up. We all see and hear things differently, that is our makeup. If you don't work on this and keep bottling everything up, you will never get rid of hindrances in your relationships and in your life.

1. If you can't stop and do this when you are angry, then go for a walk to get that anger out. Then, take the time to get quiet and ask for help to understand the situation. Come back to the person and ask to be able to hear what they are seeing and feeling, with no anger involved. Then you need to explain what you are seeing and feeling. By the way, keep the word YOU out of it. Learn to say this is what "I" am seeing, hearing, and feeling from this situation.

You will find it will help you in all areas of your life. You will feel so much better, stronger, and happier. The feeling of inadequacy and hopelessness will disappear, because you will see things in a better light. You will be able to work on your differences if you are open to make the changes to have a better relationship. You can be a better spouse, partner, parent, friend, coworker, and the best YOU ever.

This is not easy. When you learn to do it, you will find that this way of dealing with life and relationships is so much better for your whole being, especially your health. This can and does affect everything in your life. Learn to stop being the old creature of bad habits and learn to be a new and improved you. Seeking your source of power, plugging into all your inner workings – the gifts and the voice within, God, that helps you and guides you, the key to your whole life and wellbeing

Writing, journaling, prayer, meditation

All these things used in combination will help tremendously. This will get to the root of things you are dealing with in your life. Things that you wish to get rid of forever. Writing and journaling the thoughts you're thinking at that very moment are wonderful tools to use. Writing helps you to work through things. I like using this tool a lot. If you have something that is on your mind, it is always good to get your pen and paper out and write. I find that using a pen and paper are the best tool to connect to my inner thinking. The computer, I feel, just doesn't connect in a way that helps me go deep. I'm not ruling out using a computer, I just feel more connected to my feelings using a pen and paper.

For instance, when I am angry about something, I will grab my pen and pad and take off writing. Depending on my mood, I may start out writing with this depth of passion as to how I feel. It goes on my paper and I feel every word. When I start writing how I feel about something, or I need a solution to a situation, I'll start out one way and continue to write until I write through. I may start out angry about a situation, I will keep going till I get to the other end of how I feel. Most generally, once you do this and do not stop until you get to the other side, you will feel you have dumped everything out and you feel much better. For a solution to a situation, you must start out writing asking questions and continue to write whatever comes into your mind. I find that if I continue to write either fast or slow, I can come to a solution. Sometimes I may not get a complete answer to my solution, but I find it is a start. It will give me ideas to use to help me, and later I find the answers I need to resolve my situation. Just remember to write through until you feel you are released. With practice it gets easier to know when you have written enough.

There are many ways to write. You can get up first thing in the morning and just start writing. Whatever comes to your mind write it down on your paper. You will be amazed at what you may find – answers to things you didn't even think about or ask for. I truly believe that writing is a very good exercise. It just seems to bring out thoughts that would not come out on their own. I tend to write as fast as I can when I'm feeling angry upset or even when I am happy and excited about something. I will write what comes to mind and before long things start making sense.

This brings me to journaling. I believe journaling and writing can be the same, but there are different techniques in writing. Yes, we can keep them all in our journal, but there are different ways to write. Journaling can mean your daily life and what goes on. At times you may find that you are writing through some situation that needs to be resolved, or you need to get anger out of your thinking. You may say all kinds of things that you would not say to somebody's face just because you are angry. It doesn't mean anything per se, but just getting them out can make you feel so much better. I think that doing this is the right way instead of saying things like this to a person's face which you may regret afterwards. In the heat of the moment, we will say all kinds of things just to release negative angry emotions. You may not have all the facts about a situation and put your foot in your mouth after displaying your anger. The negative things you say, you won't be able to take back and may do permanent damage.

Some people can get in that place behind the steering wheel driving and say aloud words and express anger, which help get out negative thoughts. Just don't take them out on fellow drivers. We really need to get out negative emotions and the best way, I feel, is though writing. That goes for any emotion that you are going through. Don't hold them in and never deal with them. It can create all kinds of negative emotions, even sickness, as I've said earlier in this book.

Journaling is a wonderful way to write about what's happening in your lives. We can write about our life on a daily basis, not even realizing what is going on in our life, and then look back and find many things we have overlooked and just moved forward without dealing with them – things like unhappiness, or things that bother us. It shows just where we are in our thinking, and what could stand to be changed. We can find real happiness on the pages of our journal; we can find things that we don't realize are hindering us from doing the things we want to do. We can find blocks, negative patterns, or bad habits we do all the time. Journaling can show so many things we tend to neglect seeing in our lives.

I do believe journaling is a wonderful tool to help us in our lives. The only downfall to journaling is having other people look at our journals. Unfortunately, I think that is why a lot of people do not want to journal. For me, I find that journaling has become part of my life that I truly do not want to be without. Some people could even choose to journal and hide their journals, lock up their journals, or throw them away later. Whatever be your take on journaling, I find that while I'm journaling, I can get answers to questions I have – answers that may not have come to me had I not been journaling.

I like to have a pad and paper alongside of me when I do meditation or pray. I find that I get answers in meditation and prayer that need to be written down so I don't forget. I may go into meditation or prayer and feel led to stop pick up my pen and paper and start writing. Answers will come to me through meditation and prayer. There are so many ways to get answers to the questions we ask, that's why it's always a good reason to have pen and pad near you at all times so you can jot something down that comes to your mind. It's too easy to forget something that came to you in a flash moment.

I've been shown that there is a connection between all these things. Prayer, meditation, journaling, and writing will help you to get answers to all your questions, especially using them simultaneously. Through these, our voice within can come to the surface. God truly works through this combination.

These four things will help you to get to the bottom of things that hold you back like, fear, anxiety, worry, stress, depression, blocks, or whatever is hindering you.

The greatest is Love

This is a huge area we all tend to lack in. The more I research on this topic, the more I understand the saying, "love makes the world go around." People need love. I believe that every creature on this earth needs love. I see that people need the power of touch and when they aren't getting touched, they become starved for love. When a person has no love in their life, all kinds of things can go wrong, from sickness to hate. If two people stop touching each other, they become distant and other things will come into play until they hate each other or just don't want to be around each other. I'm not talking about just sex here. Although it is a big part with couples, it's not everything. I'm talking about simple little things like putting your hand on their shoulder, a hug, holding hands, putting your arm around a person, a kiss or a peek on the cheek. Or if someone is sick, some display that shows caring and says I care, I love you. This applies to all people – I think that's a part of all human relations.

Hugs, kisses, showing our love, should never stop. Building your kids up is a must in this world today. Physical contact, in a good, positive, healthy way is part of this. For instance, I give a hug hello or goodbye, or a hug for doing a great job. You can give a kind pat on the shoulder. It's great to tell them how proud you are of them. Great, positive love is much needed in this world today. I believe that evil overshadows the love God intended for us to show each other. Evil has stopped us from doing those simple acts of love humans crave. The world has turned love from the way it was intended to be into evil, because the dark side has come in to destroy love. It keeps us fearful and afraid to care the way we should.

Look at an animal. What do they love from you as their owner? You come home and they run up to you to show you love and receive love from you. You will touch them, rub their head, scratch their back, give them a hug, and acknowledge them with love. We could learn a lot from animals. People crave that kind of attention that animals desire as well. I always acknowledge my family in a hug and kiss coming and going. I want them to feel they are loved. I want to show my love. I also encourage them in everything they do and show them how proud I am of them, by praising them and singing their praises to everyone I know or meet. One thing I stay away from is saying any negative about them to others. Unconsciously, it will build up over time and create unseen barriers that can destroy your relationship.

When we become older adults, we find that the act of touch becomes less and less. Our spouse may become intolerable, which makes us never care to touch them. Then, there are older adults that lose their ability to be intimate. They have failed to realize that just by showing their love through a simple gesture of a touch can make all the difference in the world. It could also change their relationship for the better. People need to feel love. They need to see it, feel it, and be shown love in the way God wanted love to be. It makes people happier.

Even when you don't feel like showing love, it is still important for you to show love, a simple touch on the arm or hand or kind words, will release love and unkind feelings will drop away. When you give a gesture of love you will also feel the love you put out come back to you. What you sow so shall you reap. Just remember that. kindness and caring will come back into your life. I truly believe it will change your life for the better. A word of advice, physical touch needs to be done properly because it may be taken the wrong way. A fist bump, high fives, or a handshake may be the way to go with friends, the opposite sex, acquaintances, or strangers.

I was reading the book "How to Heal Your Mind" by Mona Lisa Schulz and Louise Hay. The healing spoken of in the book is all about love. It talks about loving yourself and not allowing the hurtful negative from others to destroy you. We must first learn to love ourselves and then we will have lots of love to give away. In the scripture, it says to love thy neighbor as thyself. If we don't love ourselves, then our neighbor will not get any love from us either. My son chose two Bible verses to try to live and left the rest behind. I do believe he's right. In Matthew 22: 37-39, Jesus says, "Love the Lord your God with all your heart and with all your soul, and with all your mind… and … love thy neighbor as thyself. There are no other commandments greater than these."

Two simple verses in the Bible that are so powerful, so simple, and yet so hard. There is always someone stirring up the pot to make people hate each other. It's not just today – this has happened throughout the ages. Right now, our lives are filled with hate and tearing down – from religion to politics to sports to our jobs. It is everywhere. If we could just learn these two simple verses that are the greatest commandments for life, what a world it would be. Like my son who knows the Bible inside and out and just walked away with these two scriptures, I believe that is all we need.

Let's stop judging who is right and who is wrong, because the greatest is love. Let's stop pushing whose religion is right, because the greatest is love. Let's stop letting people control what we should be doing or thinking, because the greatest is love. If we love God, ourselves, and our neighbors, then all of this fighting and taking sides would stop. That is exactly what the dark side doesn't want. It wants to stir up the pot constantly to keep us fighting, judging, hating, hurting, disrespecting, not loving ourselves or each other. It wants to keep everything negative in our lives so we feel helpless, angry and not in control. It wants us to feel worthless as human beings. We are all God's children, why is it we must feel superior over each other, and try to control each other with our thinking?

Can you open your eyes and see this for what it is? Can you let go of all this garbage and be love? Can you see these negative, condemning, judging, hateful words are from the dark side? Can you be the light of God? Can you allow happiness and love into your life? Can you love the way God intended love to be? Give it a try, one minute at a time, then an hour, a day and keep it going. Like that one little candle, full of love and light, spreads to another, and then another and so on. The light keeps the darkness out. Yes, I believe it can happen. I believe it is possible, but it begins with us. We can't look to anyone else to get us started. It is within us to have this kind of love and this kind of life. If we start choosing the love and light within, that will spill out to the world.

We are to be the light of the world. Spread your light and love and soar. Make this place a better world because you have chosen good over evil, light over darkness, love over hate, happiness over sadness, helpfulness over neglect, kindness over hurting, and praise over punches. Once we take out all the darkness in ourselves, think of how great the places we live would become.

The boss

If you really want to take this journey of changing your life, you must apply the steps I've shown you in this book. Add them to your life and into your thinking. You must get organized with your life and with your thinking. You must believe that God is showing you the way. He is directing you and guiding you in the way you need to go. You've got to want it bad enough to apply it to your life. It's not like going to work and having your boss tell you what to do. You must be your own boss. You must ask God to show you how. You need to connect to the God source that lives within, so you can do what God is showing you to do. Being boss means being connected to your power to do a great job. You will be guided every step of the way.

When your source within (God) tells you something, you need to write it down. Then do what He is telling you to do. If you met with your boss at work and were given work to do, and you walked away and didn't do any of the work, what would happen? Think about it. Nothing would get done. You would not be productive to your company and you would probably get fired.

If you are going to take charge and be the boss of your life, ask God to take control. When you connect to Him, He gives you the ideas and directions you should take. You must take notes and obey what He is telling you to do. He knows what you need to do. He will show you the right way. Let God be the CEO and He will tell you the right way to proceed with your life. Don't think evil or negative things are from God, those are negative whispers from the dark side trying to control you.

It is your place to do what He is telling you to do. Therefore, it's good to have a separate notebook for what plans God tells you to do. Have one for your journal and one for your daily schedule and the flash ideas that pop into your thoughts all day long. It is best to start the day off by going into the CEO's (God's) office and finding out what's on the agenda (through prayer, meditation and notebook.) It's the CEO's job to keep the company running smoothly. This way you will be running a top-notch company (life) and your life will be running properly – the way it should be working – and in perfect order.

If you feel in any way you don't have the time to do these things, then you can go back to the way you ran things and back to the way it wasn't working for you. That option is always there waiting for you. You have the choice to run a well-organized company (your life) or not. That is the choice that God gave each one of us. Once you start choosing to make the right changes in your life, you will be much happier and at ease, knowing that you have an experienced boss (God) running your company (your life). The things you want in your life will be known to you and you will be able to have all the things you've desired for your life.

You are not alone in your life you have everything you need to succeed in life once you learn to connect to the God source within. It is there for each of us. Learn to run your life in the way it was intended to be lived, connected to your energy, your power, your source, the God within, the Universe and everything in it.

I hope you take this information I have written in this book and apply it to your life. It was sent to me through many hours of quiet time to hear what He has called me to share. God wants you to learn how to use and apply the things that are shown to you all day long. You will wonder how you could have ever missed them. There are so many ways that God uses to speak to you. If you would just take the time to be still and hear the still small voice within, you will see the universe working with your inner and inter connections to show you how to walk on this journey in life. We are not alone. Everything works to our good and for us when we learn how it all works. Seeking through quiet time is the key.

Reference page

Definition of intuition online dictionary from Oxford and Merriam Webster

Think Yourself Rich, Joseph Murphy PH.D.,D.D. Revised by Ian D. McMahan Ph.D.2001 Rewards Books www.Penguin.com

The Power of Your Subconscious Mind- Joseph Murphy PH.D.,D.D. Copyright 2008 by Jean L. Murphy

Revocable trust and Dr. James A Boyer Published by Penguin Group

Law of the Cosmic Mind Power- Joseph Murphy Ph.D.,D.D. Revised by Ian D. McMahan

Copyright 2001 by Penguin Putnam Inc. Prentice Hall Press

Putting the Power of Your Subconscious Mind to Work- Joseph Murphy   Ph.D.,D.D.

Compiled and edited by Arthur R.Pell Ph.D. – Prentice Hall Press Published by the Penguin Group

Bible NIV- Mark7: 6-9 - Mark-8: 33- Mark -4:12- Matthew- 22:37-39

Ralph Waldo Emerson Quote- "You become what you think about all day long".

The Science of Getting What You Want- Wallace D Wattles. First published in 1910. Published by SoHo books ISN 9781441408327

Salina Rides Her Bike- Tammy Wykoff published by Outskirtspress

The Gerson Way- Charlotte Gerson with Beato Bishop, Copy right 2007-08-09-10 Sheriden Books

Cancer Healing Odyssey- Sarto Schickel- Copyright 2011- Paxdieta Books, Philadelphia

Tree of Health Center- Emotional Freedom Technique-
Debra Hollinrake

Norman Vincent Peale- Copyright-1987 by Peale Center
for Christian Living the Outreach Division of Guidepost

Joel Osteen messages-www.Joel Osteen.com- Entering
rest following labor, - Explosive Blessings

Albert Einstein- "If you always do what you've always
done, you'll always get what you've always got".

How to Heal Your Mind- Mona Lisa Schulz @ Louise Hay-
Hay House Inc. Copyright 2016 www.hayhouse.com

Epilogue

This is the most important lesson from this book. You can read any great book or go to any great seminar. You can spend lots of money on self- help information, but if you don't apply what you have learned, it will be totally worthless. You have to do what you have been shown to do. Your inner guidance can speak to you all day and night, but until you decide to apply the knowledge you have been given, your life will never change.

It is in doing that will change your life. It is in kicking out the negative whispers, the "I can't" excuse, or the failures that make you give up on yourself and keep you forever stuck in the place you don't want to be.

Teaching you to hear your voice within clearer will not work unless you are willing to listen, hear and apply what you have heard. It's time to take the necessary steps to change your life. It will change when you make the time to apply yourself and never give up.

Take time to quiet your mind to hear what you need to do. Find your peace and do what you know in your heart you need to do to have a better life. I have shared in this book ways to help you connect to your God given gifts, your inner power and source of life. Again, learn to do and apply, so these words are not lost.

This is not just another good book. It is a message to help you to take the things you've learned and apply them to your life. You are given answers to your questions, to your situations and problems. You will find that you will know it, feel it and sense it. I have given you a lot of information. My biggest hope is for you to apply this information. Remember the answers are within you.

Learn to find quiet and tune in to your source, and it will help you live the best life ever. God bless you and help you find peace, love, joy and the happiness you so deserve. May you realize all the desires of your heart are truly possible when you learn to go within.